ANATOMY OF
A BOLSHEVIK

How Marx & Lenin Explain
Obama's Grand Plan

ALEXANDER G. MARKOVSKY

ISBN 978-0-9883964-2-5 (print)
ISBN 978-0-9883964-1-8 (ePub)
ISBN 978-0-9883964-0-1 (Kindle)

Print layout and eBook editions by eBooks
by Barb for booknook.biz

To my daughter, Rebecca, the future is yours......

Preamble

My name is Alex G. Markovsky. I was born and educated in the former Soviet Union. I hold degrees in economics and political science from the University of Marxism/Leninism as well as an engineering degree from Moscow University.

Some thirty-five years ago I discovered a world infinitely freer and more prosperous that the one I came from, so for half of my life I have enjoyed freedom and affluence. For that I am grateful. To preserve this world for my children and grandchildren I wrote this book to expose the President's ideology and offer "the most accurate, predictive model of Barack Obama's behavior."

The purpose of this book is to factually and intellectually deconstruct President Obama and answer the most troubling question "Why?" Why is the President leading an assault on American values, the economy and our way of life? What is his ultimate strategic objective and what tactics is he using to accomplish it?

This book is not supposed be an unbiased assessment of the President's ideology and agenda. I do not pretend to be objective here. We all see reality through the prism of our life experience. As Shakespeare said, "Reality is not good or bad by itself; it is how we see it." It is my privilege to share with you how I see reality as viewed through the prism of Marxism/Leninism and my unique life experience.

Not to warn you about it would be dishonest.

Table of Contents

Chapter One

It Takes One to Know One

Knowing the Philosophy of Your Enemies

America: Face to Face with Liberty

To say that President Obama is a Bolshevik may sound extreme, but to someone who grew up in the former Soviet Union, and sees the world though red communist glasses, the American political landscape reveals a scary reality.

In 2008, the United States elected a radical socialist government committed to the transformation of the American capitalist free-enterprise system into an egalitarian society with a state-controlled political economy.

The great historical irony is that, unlike the Russian people who understood the perils of socialism and fought the Bolsheviks in a bloody three-year civil war that by some estimates took fifteen million lives, freedom loving Americans simply voted themselves into socialism. Communist leaders from Lenin to Brezhnev are watching from their graves in total disbelief as what proved to be impossible for the Soviet Union to accomplish with all its military might and nuclear arsenal is being enacted by a duly elected American president with the support of American voters.

As Karl Marx said, "History repeats itself, first as tragedy, second as farce." Although, the present is never a carbon copy of the past, it does provide useful parallels. So when I read Gordon Woods' brilliant book, *American Revolution*, I was struck by certain similarities between the past and present of our country. In the book's preface, Woods writes:

"Unlike the French Revolution, which had been caused by actual tyranny, the American Revolution was seen as a peculiarly intellectual and conservative affair, as something brought about not by actual oppression but by the anticipation of oppression, by reasoning and devotion to principle ...."

The key here is 'anticipation of oppression," because our country today is filled with such anticipation.

The founding fathers realized that a government, by its nature, is an institution of tyranny and designed the constitution to protect citizens from government oppression. It took many years for a large group of highly educated and dedicated people to convince the American electorate that American Idealism and our social and economic policies required dramatic revisions. They persuaded a significant sector of the population that free individuals cannot govern themselves effectively and that government must play a greater role in order to control the economy and engineer "social justice."

This agenda brought with it subsequent changes to the moral principles that guided this country for more than 200 years.

The major challenge facing the American people today is to understand the danger to our democracy from socialist radicals who refuse to accept that the ills of society cannot be fixed by the government.

If the American people do not accept this fundamental,

American Democracy may not live for much longer. The current socialist administration has enacted a series of laws whose cumulative effect, unless repealed, will change this country forever.

As the 2010 congressional elections demonstrated, the American people do get it. However, the challenges of taking America back from the political elite are enormous. The people of California and New York, who are heavily dependent on government subsidies, voted in the same people who bankrupted their states so as to ensure a continued culture of entitlements. In those states where professional politicians were voted out of office, they were defeated by a slight majority. The Left has amassed enormous power with a constituency that possesses organizational skills and very substantial financial strength.

The isolation from the world's turmoil that America has enjoyed over the last 250 years has inhibited our capacity to understand the vulnerabilities of our democracy and the fragility of our constitutional restraints, which in turn has corroded our values and impaired our ability to recognize the danger before us.

If this government has its way we will become the unfortunate generation, dying bankrupt and telling our children and grandchildren, "Work hard and pay, pay, pay forever for our utopian dream."

Will America in "anticipation of oppression" use "reasoning and devotion to principle" to resist the power of demagoguery and lies, detect the danger, repair itself and continue on its path to what Alexander Hamilton described as the path to "greater perfection and happiness that mankind has yet seen?"

That is what this book is about.

The Way It Was

As you already know, I was born in a country that no longer exists, the Union of Soviet Socialist Republics (USSR). Sometimes it is hard to comprehend that a huge empire, that extended over eleven time zones with a dozen or so satellite countries, could cease to function. Once perceived as an economic and military powerhouse, the Soviet Union collapsed like a house of cards.

It also proved once again that empires and economic powers start rotting from the inside due to, as Karl Marx said, internal contradictions. The lesson here is that behind the veils of propaganda and official pronouncements, things are not always what they seem.

The Soviet Union was built on utopian ideology, and when the ideology was pulled out from under the monolith, there was nothing to hold it together. My father predicted the collapse long before it took place. But unfortunately did not live to see its demise; he passed away just a few years short of this historic event.

Like millions of Russian citizens, my father dedicated his life to building socialism. He defended his country during the Second World War. He rose through the professional and party ranks to become the director of a large construction company as well as a high-ranking member of the Communist Party. Party membership was a way of life for him, the way to support his family and to survive in a highly ideological and often dangerous environment.

All Soviet-era managers had to be members of the Communist Party. My father joked that a rabbi in a synagogue must be a member of the party because such a position of authority would never be held by a non-Party individual. His civilian post and his position in the Communist Party provided a host of privileges, such as a higher salary, a better apartment, a company car, and access to special stores where high-ranking members could obtain goods unavailable to the general population at a fraction of the price.

Being a high-ranking member of the party ensured a relatively good life and a secure future for his children—to the extent that anything or anybody could be secure in the Soviet Union, given the constant and real fear of denunciation to the KGB, and the possibility of being taken at a moment's notice to the KGB's torture chambers and executed or exiled to the archipelago of jails and labor camps all over the country.

I grew up knowing that my father hated the bastards who ran the Soviet State, the Communist party, and also ran his life. He never believed in their "working people's paradise," and he always treated the arrangement as a marriage of convenience.

Living with the corrupt system has been the subject of many American popular books and movies, but for many, like my father, it was a real-life dilemma. During the day my father and his like-minded comrades enthusiastically supported every party initiative, be it a five-year plan or condemnation of a new Solzhenitsyn book that none of them had ever read. By day, they were united in their quest to defeat world imperialism, Chinese revisionism, and to "plant the red flag over the planet." At night, they shared anecdotes about Khrushchev's stupidity, Brezhnev's illiteracy and the futility of communist orthodoxy.

My father enjoyed the period of political thawing that took place after the death of Joseph Stalin, and sometimes his humor would take the form of sarcasm. I recall an incident that occurred one weekend when he took me to visit a construction site located across the street from KGB headquarters. When we were leaving the site, a KGB general was coming out of the building.

"Hi, Gregory, how are you doing?" the general called to my father. Before my father could answer the general complained, "You are blocking our sunlight"—referring to the new building under construction

"That is only fair," my father replied, "You people have been blocking me from seeing the sunlight all my life!" They both laughed.

"You know, Gregory, you are very lucky. During the Stalin era, a remark like that, even under the best of circumstances, would get you sent to Siberia."

"I know," my father said. "Back then I would have tried to keep my mouth shut."

I guess my father was always torn between prudence and vanity. All his life he had navigated so skillfully between Soviet ideology and his own reality that it would have been difficult for an outsider to comprehend the depth of duplicity and antagonism he carried over the years.

As his son, I grew up watching him don his communist persona to begin his workday; then shed it again at night when surrounded by his family and friends. From this, I developed a healthy understanding of and skepticism for the socialist state. One day his philosophical dilemma manifested itself in a most unexpected way.

The Philosophy of Your Enemies

I vividly remember that twilight evening at the end of the hot summer of 1964. My father returned home after a late meeting at the Communist Party headquarters and asked me to accompany him to his home office, "We need to talk," he said in his professorial tone, which bordered at times on condescension, "I have arranged for you to go to the University of Marxism-Leninism to study political science."

"Are you out of your mind, Dad?" I protested. "Why would you want me to waste my time on that communist crap?"

"The Führer," which was what he called the secretary of the City Branch of the Communist Party, "has approved your candidacy. It is arranged."

I was shocked to discover that he was completely serious about this. He continued talking, trying to convince me that this was a big deal for a Jewish boy, since the University accepted only "Aryan master race candidates," meaning applicants with a stellar proletarian background, and that "no Jew shall apply."

I was incredulous. "Then by all means I shall be proud," I said, thick with the sarcasm that made hypocrisy palatable to many generations of Jewish suffering, "to study utopian theories and political economy, which I have a difficulty understanding due to its complete lack of logic, and I shall appreciate the honor of graduating in the Art of Demagoguery and Lies."

My father did not smile at my mockery, although I'd heard him utter similar disdain when conversing with his friends. Instead, his next words came at me with the force of the Bolsheviks' hammer and sickle. They became deeply embedded in my thinking.

"Son, that's what the Communist philosophy is all about. *If you want to survive, you have to understand the philosophy of your enemies.*" His blue eyes were ice cold. "*One should never underestimate the boundless power of demagoguery and lies. It moves nations.*"

His voice trembled for a moment and then it was over. He turned around and walked out of the room. This explicit message coming from the mouth of a high ranking communist who had survived the upheavals of Bolshevism —the terror, economic destruction, famine and the un- limited power of the state—could not be disregarded.

The Highest Art

Years later, my father demonstrated how well he knew his enemies and how masterfully he could maneuver himself out of an extremely difficult situation. The day of reckoning arrived in November 1975, when my father had to sign consent to allow me, his son, to emigrate to Israel.

There seemed to be no way out of it and no acceptable solution to the quandary. If he signed the papers, he would be viewed as a coward allowing his son to betray the motherland. As a result, he would lose his Party membership, his job, and the respect and prestige he enjoyed among his colleagues. He would also be denounced by his comrades and become *persona non grata*. He would lose everything he had worked for all his life, including his sizable pension.

On the other hand, if he did not sign the papers he was still considered the father of a traitor. The result would be the same; there was no way around it.

Or was there? My father requested a meeting with the Party's City Committee.

"Comrades," he said, "I am suffering a personal tragedy, but the issue we are facing is a lot greater than me. It touches all of us and raises serious questions about the communist future of our country. My son has been seduced by imperialist propaganda and has decided to leave his motherland and emigrate to Israel. How did *we* miss that? I take complete responsibility for what has happened. I am his father and the blame is mine alone.

"However, I thought I did all the right things. My son went to a Soviet school. He was a member of Komsomol (the communist party youth organization). He graduated from a Soviet university, and I even sent him to study Marxism at the University of Marxism-Leninism. Where did *we* go wrong with the way we are preparing a new generation to take over the wheel of our beloved socialist country?"

Cleverly and adroitly, my father demonstrated the highest art of the communists' demagoguery and turned it against them. What was the outcome?

Nothing really happened, nothing at all. I was allowed to leave the country and my father kept his job and his Communist Party post for a few more years until his retirement. However, seeing his skillful maneuver, I understood how he had survived and used his knowledge to become the master of the game.

Needless to say, I attended the university and, to my surprise, I liked it. I studied political science and economics. I had access to communist publications usually restricted to a very narrow circle of readers. The university turned out to be the only place in the Soviet Union where I could exercise my constitutional right to free speech—with some restrictions of course.

Thus, I gained an understanding of American democracy, economy, and politics, while my studies endowed me with a deep understanding of Marxist-Leninism as a political philosophy, methods of achieving political objectives, political economy, and above all, the Bolsheviks' thinking.

The most important element of this knowledge was the realization that Marxists are dogmatic and predictable; they go strictly by the book, and for someone who understands Marxism-Leninism, the outcome of issues could be foreseen.

Equipped with this knowledge I successfully managed my emigration ordeal through eight years of rejection, including numerous KGB interrogations and arrests. In December of 1975, I finally got out of the "big zone," which was how Soviet political prisoners called the Soviet Union, versus a "small zone," which was how they referred to the labor camps.

Unlike many of my friends I was never hurt, prosecuted, or incarcerated throughout that period. Contrary to the treatment of all other *refuzniks* (a Russian word for those who dared to apply for emigration and were turned down by the authorities), I was not publicly denounced and expelled from the State University.

I was allowed to successfully complete my education, graduating as a civil-structural engineer, following my studies at the University of Marxism-Leninism where I received degrees in economics and political science. Meanwhile, I worked for various State engineering companies until the day before I left the country. I have no doubt that, without this knowledge, I would not be standing here with you. I would have been dead a long time ago, starved in one of the Soviet concentration camps or disappeared in one of the country's psychiatric clinics.

I am sure my father is looking down at me from the heavens and smiling, yet I do not believe he realized at the time the long-reaching value of his advice.

Armed with his advice plus the knowledge and experience gained during my life in the Soviet Union, I observe the political landscape through my red communist glasses and see a reality that most Americans cannot see and an encroaching future Americans do not want to see. So my fellow Americans, get my red communist glasses on right now and see what I see:

I have seen this future and it does not work.

Sheep are Made to be Groomed

I used to believe that people were divided into two categories—those who have a paycheck and those who don't. Now that I have made millions I know that people are divided into two categories—those who need a paycheck and those who don't.

I have little sympathy for the so-called "poor people." I have been poor. I came to this country in May of 1976 with five dollars in my pocket, not knowing a word of English. I succeeded; but my story is not unusual. To the contrary, there are millions of immigrants who come to this country every year. They all have their stories of poverty, suffering, sometimes humiliation, despair, and optimism. For most of them, optimism wins. They have worked hard and succeeded in their American dream. That was to be expected.

However, what I learned in my very first week after arriving in New York from my fellow countrymen was not expected. I learned two very important things about this country. First, in this the richest country in the world, millions of people were classified as poor. Second, Americans had a peculiar definition of poverty that was vastly different than what a reasonable person might expect.

I always believed that poverty was a state of having little to no money, and few or no material possessions. To my amazement poor people in this country had cars, government subsidized apartments, food stamps, free medical care, welfare checks, and a variety of generous social programs that provided decent and in many instances, a pretty luxurious living. Which confirms an old Jewish adage: a man doesn't know that he is poor until he is told so.

"One does not have to work to enjoy a good living," I was told. What you have to do, "is to be poor and the government will take care of you," I was informed in confidence my very first week in America.

My Russian friends living in Brooklyn were collecting welfare checks and food stamps from three neighboring States: New York, New Jersey, and Connecticut. All one needed to do was to provide a home address of his friends living in those states. The friends in turn, provided a home address in Brooklyn to be eligible for the benefits in New York.

The government, I learned, would also pay for taking care of the elderly. So you take care of my mother and I will take care of your mother. Needless to say, nobody was providing any care and neither parent needed to be taken care of in the first place. I do not remember all those insane programs, I just remember there were many of them and politicians were going out of their way to come up with new ones.

This whole charade reminded me of how beggars behave. As soon as you advance some change to one of them, a howling swarm surrounds you demanding every penny you have.

In the case of the government the beggars usually get what they want, and more.

Furthermore, if you are not really a lazy bastard, you can supplement your generous government benefits by working for cash, which in New York is very common, even today. Food stamps served as a second currency. One could buy a used car, furniture, appliances, etc, all with the currency of food stamps. Eventually some of the "poor" managed to save enough money to buy small businesses like delis, restaurants, shoe repair stores, or taxi medallions for operating a taxi service. I knew someone who never worked a day in his life who opened a big jewelry store on 47th street.

Life in America was great and the opportunities to make money off the government were abundant. It was especially true for my countrymen who were born and raised under the socialist regime. They could adapt easily to this familiar lifestyle, which basically meant taking advantage of government handouts and the profound incompetence of government employees.

I use the Russian community only as an example since I was well familiar with it. There should be no doubt, however, that the Russians did not invent these tricks. Nor were they alone in practicing them. Other communities like the Italians, Chinese, Vietnamese, and other minorities used similar tricks to enrich themselves at the expense of the US taxpayers. And why not? As my Russian friend said, "God made sheep to be groomed."

I knew several African-American couples who had children but would not get married, so the woman could apply for government assistance as a single mother with, as one woman told me, "a few children." She said it as if she did not even know how many children she had. The more children, the more money she would collect in the form of various benefits.

I remember walking down Broadway thinking; "if one wants to drive a car he/she needs to pass a test and get a license. But if you want to have a child, you can have it: no test, and no license is required. Doesn't it make sense that anyone who wants to have a child must offer proof of their mental stability and financial ability to support a child? Sure, the liberals would say something about human rights. But what about the rights of humans? What about me? I could not understand why should I pay for someone else's child, born out of wedlock? Where is the father? And what about those fathers who disappear? Why does society have to pay for their indiscretions and lack of responsibility? If society pays for illegitimate children it makes sense for women to have as many as possible to live off the children.

Why should I have to pay for irresponsible parents? Or even worse, why should I pay for illegal schemes? When it comes down to individual rights versus the rights of society, the individual always wins and society picks up the bill. And when I says "society," very often that means "we the people" who have jobs and pay taxes, must keep picking up the bills during this "child's" life.

Americans call it social justice. In this version of justice, if you are an unemployed female drug addict that has five children from five different men, you are entitled to a comfortable house or at least a three bedroom apartment, welfare checks, food stamps and all other government benefits because 'the children should not suffer' due to their mother's irresponsible behavior. However, if you are a responsible parent, and have a family and two kids and work hard to support your family, the government takes half of what you earned so as to support the lazy drug addict.

I must confess that I had a very difficult time relating to this type of justice. Raised in a communist country I saw the world differently, some might say primitively. In my "unjust" primitive world; someone who does not work does not eat. Perhaps, with the exception of those who cannot work; the chronically ill, handicapped, and the elderly, able body individuals should not be supported by society. That was my subjective opinion. However, this capitalist world had its own rules. To live in New York one had to be either very rich or poor. The rich don't need a paycheck; and the poor don't either because they have government handouts. For anyone in the middle, who actually needed to earn a paycheck, life was very difficult. Defending the poor became a lucrative business in of itself. Black leaders, or so called civil rights leaders, like Jesse Jackson and Al Sharpton became millionaires defending the poor and blackmailing the government and private industries to award contracts to so-called minority businesses.

I remember prominent democrats Bella Abzug and Daniel Patrick Moynihan marching down Fifth Avenue before the 1976 elections promising more government help to support the needy. No wonder Moynihan won the senate seat from New York.

In this light, it is hard to dispute Karl Marx: "It is not the consciousness of [people] that determines their existence, but their social existence that determines their consciousness."

It may sound ironic, but this is a central postulate of contemporary conservative philosophy. New York democrats, however, practicing their liberal philosophy, still believe that it is the government's policies that influence the people's consciousness.

Democrats have been piling up social programs for the poor trying to engineer their social existence. However, in the process, they developed a culture of parasitism and dependency among the aid recipients. The State's constant enabling of new programs and new initiatives breeds a

new type of citizenry that doesn't look to sustain themselves, but instead looks to the State for handouts.

It is impossible for a democratic society to ignore the
so called "less fortunate" for a very simple reason—they do
vote. The objective reality of democratic society requires
the elected representatives to get re-elected.

I well remember Karl Marx's prophesy that capitalism
is not sustainable as an economic system and would inevitably be replaced by socialism. It was not hard to imagine
the transformation of American society to a government-
controlled economy with a continuing increase in social
programs. Ironically, it was not so much that the capitalist
economy was not sustainable. The problem, rather, was the
sustainability of democracy. The more people getting benefits from the government, the more people voted for that
government.

The very fact that the government draws power and
legitimacy from social programs is inherently immoral and
undermines the very system the country was based upon.
It turns American democratic Idealism, historic values and
traditions on their head and has greatly contributed to the
economic decline and moral decay of society.

The topic of how millions of Americans are living off
government handouts would require a separate book. I am
just making the point that in order to achieve a comfortable
living in this country a person does not necessarily have to
work hard, if at all.

I had to decide: Which side of this social "Great
Divide" did I want to be on? The receiving end or was I

going to be the one picking up the bill?" Is it going to be the Left side or the Right side?

Eventually, I made my choice; I took the Right side and was taken for the ride of my life. And, what a ride it was.

I had my Dreams

My journey took me from rags to riches, from riches to rags and from rags to riches again. At one time, early after I arrived in the United States, I still had my own dreams. I was dreaming big. I was young, ambitious and extremely confident. There was only one problem; I did not speak English.

I was working during the day, and at night and on weekends, I studied English at Columbia University. I was also desperately looking for a suitable capitalist "exploiter of the working people" who would exploit my talents and knowledge for profit and personal enrichment. I was prepared to work for a "miserable capitalist salary," as communist propaganda called American wages. Unfortunately, America was going through an economic downturn and jobs were very scarce.

I got a job working as a window washer on skyscrapers and as a house painter.

Being an experienced engineer but unable to use my skills was an especially painful and frustrating experience. Luckily, years ago, my father insisted that I work at one of his construction sites as a laborer learning different construction trades as a precondition to his hiring me for a lower managerial position. The skills came in handy in the highly competitive engineering environment. So, I, the experienced civil-structural engineer had to work as a house painter and skyscraper window-washer. I could now afford spaghetti at my favorite Italian joint but not the meatballs that went with it.

It was there, washing windows in offices and painting multimillion dollar apartments that I for the first time realized the enormity of opportunities available to a poor emigrant from the Soviet Union. It was there I discovered the invariable capitalist truth; *inequality is a locomotive of progress.*

I continued to look for a better job. One day my perseverance paid off. I got an offer to assume an engineering position at the construction of a Nuclear Power Plant in Bay City, Texas with Brown & Root of Houston. I got a compensation package I could not even dream of. It was best day of my life.

Several years later, I was lead engineer with an international engineering company. I owned a house and the latest model car. In the early 1980s, during the recession I was unemployed, I lost a house and was unable to replace my car's tires or pay rent for an apartment. I started in the real estate development business and was making very good money. One day during S&L crisis, the lender went under and took me with them. I was back in poverty.

Then one day, everything changed again when I was offered a great position with a major international energy company. Over time I was promoted to a senior management position.

When management got tired of my business ideas, I was told, "If you are so smart, why don't you do it yourself? I took their advice, got on a plane to Moscow and ten days later signed my first $10 million contract.

I have been in; I have been out. I have been up, I have been down. I have been poor and I have been wealthy.

In 2008 the business slowed to a stop. I am still waiting for the next page. However, by then I could afford to wait.

From time to time I couldn't help but think how my life would have evolved if I had taken the Left side of the social "Great Divide"? The only thing I know for certain is that it would have led me inevitably to voting for Democrats and donating stacks of food stamps to Obama's reelection campaign.

I went on with my life confident that America would survive during my life time and there would be enough life in capitalism and the American democracy for the next 100 years or so. I have been proved wrong and socialism reached the American shores a lot sooner than I thought.

The Future Arrived and It Was not Exactly what We Expected

In November 5, 2008, the day after the Presidential elections I walked into the sales office of a luxury high rise condominium located at 2727 Kirby in Houston, Texas where I had a contract to buy a $3 Million dollar condo.

"The Bolsheviks have taken the White House. The country is toast," I told the sales manager. "I am bailing out of my contract."

There was something depressing and ironic that the bloody Bolshevik revolution in Russia took place on November 7, 1917 and now, 91 years later, almost to the day, we were facing a bloodless revolution in the United States. I guess the world has changed for the better.

During my first year in New York, I had a recurring nightmare that the Bolsheviks took over the United States and the New York City communist party office set up their headquarters in the Empire State Building. A huge red flag was planted on the top of the building. Roaring cheers and screams of joy swept through 34th street as people were celebrating capitalism's demise. It was like my worst fears coming true: I was going back to the future.

Patrick Henry said, "I have but one lamp by which my feet are guided; and that is the lamp of experience. I know of no way of judging of the future but by the past."

Having been raised in the Soviet Union, I knew socialism firsthand and could spot a Bolshevik when I saw one. What I saw did not paint a pretty picture: American values were undergoing a conversion that could result in wholesale constitutional and social changes. The country was facing ambiguous choices and uncertain outcomes.

What was certain, we were entering a period of political upheaval and a protracted economic downturn. As the measures culminating in revolutionary changes of society and the economy get implemented, the effect will be detrimental. Private investment will dry up, as capitalists do not invest in uncertainty, and certainly not in a political economy, thereby causing protracted economic stagnation. Should President Obama get reelected to a second term, the downturn would most certainly transition into protracted economic paralysis.

It was inconceivable that the greatest civilization, greatest economy and military power on Earth was going to self-destruct. You may recall the answer that Benjamin Franklin, gave at Independence Hall in Philadelphia after the Constitutional Convention of 1787 ended, when Mrs. Powel asked "Well, Doctor, what we have got, a republic or a monarchy? Franklin responded, "A republic, if you can keep it." The 2008 elections created a reasonable doubt that America will be able to preserve its unique form of democracy and survive a massive assault on its institutions.

For someone who escaped socialism thirty two years earlier, it was a heartbreaking moment. Were Americans buying into this intellectual dream of a social paradise?

Was Karl Marx indeed right when he predicted that socialism will eventually replace capitalism? Is the USA, United States of America, converting into USSA, United Socialist States of America?

And, what about me and my children and grandchildren? I was reminded of an old Russian man that I met at the dirty, rundown St. George Hotel in Brooklyn in 1976. He was very happy to meet a fellow émigré countryman and after a drink or two in a nearby café he told me a fascinating story of his life and constant run from communism.

The man, whom I will call Victor, was born in Russia before the Bolshevik revolution, in the city of Samara to a family of prosperous industrialists. He was the youngest and had two brothers and a sister. Victor was ten years old when the Bolsheviks took power and unleashed their brand of fairness and justice. All the property and possessions of his father were expropriated by the working people's State. The family escaped to Latvia with what little they could salvage and with the help of former business associates his father opened an import-export business.

By 1939, the family had prospered again. His brothers and sister got married and a small crowd of grandchildren made the parents very happy. But in 1939, the Red Army "liberated" Latvia. It happened so fast that Victor was the only one who managed to escape. The rest of his family was arrested by the NKVD, the Russian secret police, and eventually perished in the Gulag. Victor was lucky enough to reach the Chinese city of Harbin with its big Russian community. Victor got a job with China Eastern Railway, married and tried to adjust to his new environment.

However, all hell broke loose again in 1945 when the Red Army occupied Harbin. This time he decided to run to the other side of the planet, so there would be no chance for the Reds to get him ever again. So, he traveled to Cuba. In 1959, Fidel Castro seized power in Cuba and Victor fled to the United States. He lost his wife soon after they arrived in the U.S. They never had children. Victor was ending his life alone, old, destitute and sick.

Now in 2008, I thought of Victor, and I wondered: Although it was unlikely that he was still alive, if he had survived, where would he run to now?? Was this the end of the road?

I thought about whether my destiny was going to be like Victor's; but Cuba was not an option.

Chapter Two

American Neo-Bolshevik

"Debauch the currency to overturn the basis of society." Lenin

Historical Inevitability

Often, I've been asked, "What is the difference between socialists and Bolsheviks? A common interpretation of socialism is, "An economic system characterized by public ownership and centralized planning of the economy." The essence of socialism is the distribution of wealth in a so-called "fair and equitable way" by the people (read: "by the government"). Socialism is, by definition, democratic; it is an economic as well as a political democracy. Socialists advocate for the redistribution of wealth through the democratic process via taxation and government regulation.

Bolshevism is defined by its methods of achieving the prime socialist objective of the redistribution of wealth. The Bolsheviks' strategy and tactics emanate from the political and economic theories of German economist Karl Marx, as further developed by Russian professional revolutionary, Vladimir Lenin. In accordance with Lenin's theories, economic and social justice must be accomplished by force with the imposition of a "dictatorship of the proletariat"

The Bolsheviks, which in Russian means "majority," were a radical faction of the Marxist Russian Social Democratic Labor Party (RSDLP), which split from the Menshevik "minority" faction at the Second Party Congress in 1903. They ultimately became the Communist Party of the Soviet Union.

To the Bolsheviks, Marxism is not just another political and economic theory. It is the supreme gospel, an infallible

truth that prophesies universal social justice. The cornerstone of Russian Bolshevism was a conviction that
capitalism is evil; it ought to be destroyed and replaced
with socialism and later, with Communism (the final stage
of socialism).

In 1814 French astronomer Pierre-Simon Laplace came
up with a theory of how to predict the future. He theorized
that if you "know all forces that set nature in motion, and
all positions of all items, of which nature is composed,"
together with all the laws of physics and chemistry, then
"Nothing would be uncertain and the future, just like the
past, would be present" before your eyes. Karl Marx
applied this idea to society and history and developed a
theory of "historical inevitability."

The Bolsheviks believed that Communism represents
the vanguard of history and its triumph over capitalism is
inevitable. It is a historical inevitability, and therefore,
should be enforced upon a population incapable of
appreciating its greatness or understanding the concept of
economic equality and the fairness of wealth distribution.
Consequently, there is no need for a messy democratic
process when the outcome is preordained.

As I write this, generations of Americans have grown
up who have no memory of Bolshevism. American schools
hardly even mention this tragic period of world history.
But for someone who has personal experience and
memories of this period, the situation could not be clearer.
The President's agenda, his strategy, his tactics and his
methods of accomplishing his objectives can be traced

directly back to the teachings of Marx and Lenin. The body of circumstantial evidence is overwhelming.

Philosophy of Poverty

During the 2008 Presidential elections, John McCain said about Obama, "I am not questioning his patriotism, I am questioning his judgment." McCain was wrong. Obama is blessed with sound analytical judgment, but his ideology and his agenda, raised doubts among the American people about his commitment to American Idealism and, therefore, must be questioned.

Ever since Obama's inauguration, the overwhelming majority of the media (I can think of only a few exceptions) has been enamored with the President, comparing him to John Adams, Thomas Jefferson, and Abraham Lincoln. Harvard historian James T. Kloppenberg has gone so far as to call him a philosopher president.

If the President is a philosopher, then the philosophy he is promulgating is Karl Marx's "The Philosophy of Poverty" (which is how 19th Century French politician, philosopher, and socialist Pierre-Joseph Proudhon described Karl Marx's theories in his book, "System of Economical Contradictions: or, "The Philosophy of Poverty"[1]).

Obama's agenda reads as if it came straight out of the University of Marxism-Leninism. There is nothing new here but the striking parallels between the Russian Bolsheviks and Obama's administration; both utterly

convinced of their own uncompromising righteousness
and fanatic belief in economic equality, and both equally
obsessed with power and control.

The President exhibits the attributes of Bolshevism, having a propensity for autocratic rule and disdain for democratic process. He created a shadow government consisting of thirty left-wing radicals, former and current members of the communist party, anti-business and anti-gun activists, first amendment opponents, radical homo-sexuals; that can best be described as a stinking bouquet of intellectual garbage one can find on the outskirts of every society. Those hand-picked appointments of incompetent but loyal czars were intended to circumvent the Congress' approval and scrutiny. Although, Obama called them czars in reality they are more akin to Bolshevik commissars— overseeing their respective departments, making sure the President's destructive socialist policies are implemented to the letter.

We all remember President Obama's "We Can't Wait" tour when he engaged in a campaign tactic to pressure Congress into passing his legislative agenda. As a typical Bolshevik, Obama feels a lot more comfortable talking than doing; and using intimidation rather than negotiation. In essence, he was saying he could not wait for the democratic process to work. Governing by executive orders as an alter-native to achieving consensus has become the President's mode of operation.

In many instances by extending his use of executive

orders Obama bluntly violates the Constitution and the rule of law. The most recent examples are Obama's decision to relieve work requirements for welfare recipients in violation of the existing legislation and to block deportation of some young illegal immigrants in violation of the US immigration law.

When the President can ignore the law, and replace legislating with executive orders, we are no longer governed by the rule of law. We will then be no better than a communist regime or banana republic.

The President is using his authority to challenge the guiding principles of our nation. American Idealism embraces national debate on both sides of the issue. Although the process may seem a messy and procrastinating affair, it is itself an expression of the strength of American democracy—not a weakness as the President and his supporters perceive. The separation of powers outlined in the Constitution imposes constraints that are permanent features of our system of governing and that characterize a mature democratic process.

The Neo-Bolshevik's impatience with the process and generally scant respect for democracy, gives President Obama no incentive to work on legislation and move it through Congress. Augmented by "historical inevitability," when unable to pass his legislation through the democratic system of governing, the President instead prefers to take an "easy pass" through the highway of American democracy; he ignores it. He treats the Constitution like a traffic light with all three colors on at once. So he chooses the one he likes.

Why? Because what the President is trying to accomplish, is the "right thing to do." "Right thing to do!" "Right thing to do!" Joyously declares the President over and over again, demonstrating a cynical disregard for one of the most fundamental aspects of American democracy:

> *The American people have the constitutional right to be*
> *wrong but the President does not have the right to*
> *define for them what is right.*

In this society "what is right" is determined by our duly elected representatives in Congress. Perhaps the media and democrats who unequivocally support the President's actions may think that the founding fathers could not envision a genius like Barack Obama in the White House and failed to address this extraordinary circumstance in the Constitution. Somewhat like a constitutional "Force Majeure" clause. Thus, this minor imperfection of the United States Constitution shall not be an impediment to "do the right thing." This progressive interpretation of the US constitution would, no doubt, be appreciated in Moscow and Beijing.

Some of us recall that when the concept of "The right thing to do" was applied in Russia by the Bolsheviks, it caused twenty million Soviet citizens murdered in labor camp and prisons by order of Lenin and Stalin. Millions more were starved to death building the promised egalitarian paradise. The autocracies that reject the imposition of limits on their authority and use "efficient" ways to arrive at "what is right" end up with lies, starvation and blood. No exception.

Disastrously, there was a bloody reasoning behind the Bolsheviks' terror. The reasoning was, and still is, that we [Bolsheviks] are right, we know that we are. The advanced theory of Marxism-Leninism tells us that what we are set to do is a historical inevitability, it is going to happen anyway. Therefore the people who disagree with us are nothing more than human garbage that prevents us from achieving our bright future; they need to be destroyed.

The world has changed since 1917 and nobody is planning on physically destroying their opponents. But we see the logic here. The Neo-Bolsheviks feel justified in subverting those democratic principles which prevent them from the speedy implementation of their agenda. Once launched on a course, they will not abandon it, regardless of the efforts or the sacrifice. They fanatically believe that the future belongs to them and that they can discard the tragic lessons of their predecessors as mistakes made in the process of implementation of progressive ideas. This time they will get "the right thing" right.

I am not a Marxist

Republicans criticize the President for unrestrained spending, high unemployment, and the high cost of gasoline, portraying him as misguided and in-over-his-head, as he tries ineffectively to stabilize the economy. They label the President's policies a colossal failure and offer boiler-plate presidential campaign accusations. Although the President's record makes him vulnerable, tough-sounding rhetoric is no substitute for a realistic assessment of his agenda and policies, nor is it a substitute for the facts.

Webster's Dictionary defines failure as a lack of success. Facts demonstrate that this President has been *very* successful in implementing his legislative agenda.

It is Obama's agenda, consisting of policies snipped from the Bolshevik past and resurrected from the garbage dump of history, that are so deeply troubling.

For the political pundits who evaluate the President's actions from the standpoint of conventional politics, his actions look so bizarre that they mystify his critics and supporters alike.

He says he wants to balance the budget but is running the deficit to unsustainable levels and insists on spending even more. He is talking about American economic competitiveness but is spending billions of dollars on green energy that costs the consumers and businesses substantially more than conventional sources, making American products and services less competitive. He is talking about energy independence but he prevents oil drilling and building the Keystone pipeline that would bring cheap Canadian oil to Texas refineries. He says he wants to reduce unemployment but prevents Boeing from opening a new facility in South Carolina. He says he supports Israel but wants her to live within its 1967 borders; he says Iran should not obtain a nuclear weapon but does nothing to prevent it.

There is more: He created the Simpson-Bowles Commission and then refused to endorse its deficit-reducing proposals. He engaged in long negotiations on the debt ceiling without putting forward his own specific plan to the public. President Obama could have come forth with deficit-reduction plans at any point in his presidency, but he didn't. He wants to work with Republicans but calls them an enemy of the people. He demands Congress sign the so-called "Jobs Bill" that includes an allocation of 140 Billion dollars for rebuilding and maintaining infrastructure, while after spending 800 billion dollars of the first stimulus package on so-called shovel-ready projects that turned out to be not so "shovel-ready," he knows his proposal is unacceptable to the Republicans and would, under no circumstance, pass the House. The list of inconsistencies can go on and on.

The President, who during his election campaign told Americans that he is capable of working across the aisle, cannot find political common ground with anybody outside of his Democratic base. Obama's administration is in a permanent state of war—with the Republicans about the future of this country; with the business community about taxes and regulations; with the States about health care, oil and gas drilling, border security and voting rights; and with the Catholic Church about church policies on abortion and contraception, just to name a few.

The critics of the President portray him as out of touch,

incompetent, and misguided. The stark reality, and what Republican leaders have failed thus far to recognize as an immutable fact, is that the President may be out of touch and incompetent but he and his supporters are not misguided; they are guided by the ideology of Marxism/ Leninism.

As a result, the Republicans keep emphasizing the obvious over the important. The President should be judged by what he does, as well as by what he says—not by the promises he makes but the promises he keeps. Obama's almost daily speeches are saturated with Marxist ideology and offer us a unique glimpse at his objectives and strategy.

Although the President denies he is a socialist, such as his assertion that "Contrary to the claims of some of my critics and some of the editorial pages, I am an ardent believer in the free market," Obama sounds as credible as when Karl Marx earnestly stated, "If anything is certain, it is that I myself am not a Marxist."

There is a simple explanation for the President's actions: our president lives in a different world; the world of Marxist Dialectical materialism, where change is the product of a constant conflict between opposites arising from the internal contradictions inherent in all events, ideas, and movements.

So, as long as he sees the world as a conflict of opposing forces, Obama will seek conflict as the process leading to achieving his strategic objectives. It is important to understand that he is not just incapable of conflict resolution; he is manufacturing conflicts in order to shore up his base and disparage political opponents. In the mind of a Bolshevik, anything less than 100 percent support is betrayal.

He confuses political discourse with the state of warfare. In classic Bolshevik style, he uses intimidation tactics and issues direct threats to his political opponents. In October 2010, before the November elections, when Obama spoke with Eddie Sotelo, a host of Univision, he issued a warning, "We're gonna punish our enemies and we're gonna reward our friends who stand with us on issues that are important to us." And then referring to the Republicans, he added, "Those aren't the kind of folks who represent our core American values." It reverberates with Lenin's motto during the Russian civil war, "Who is not with us, is against us."

After suffering a staggering defeat at the polls in November 2010, the President promised cooperation and a willingness to compromise. But at the same time, he has never missed an opportunity to enhance his eminence by denigrating his political opponents. He is constantly seeking domination in a way that is more an attribute of a totalitarian ruler than that of a consensus builder, which is a distinctive feature of democracy.

Victory at any cost becomes the only acceptable outcome of political discourse.

We all remember too well his arrogant pronouncement, "I won." Those who dare to disagree with him are enemies of the people and shall be destroyed. In this confrontational environment, there is no room for statesmanship, cooperation, and compromise. As a matter of fact, Marxism-Leninism defines compromise as a "solution equally unacceptable for all parties involved." Unable to find a middle ground between total victory and total defeat, Obama has worked himself into a deadlock.

Incapable and unwilling to compromise, the President will continue to emulate the Bolsheviks' tactics and rhetoric by exploiting class warfare, civil disobedience, and riots; reaching out to minorities and intellectuals, dividing the nation along racial lines and income brackets to implement "Change." This tactic was condemned by another former Senator from Illinois, Abraham Lincoln, who famously said, "A house divided against itself cannot stand." While the American house has been divided, our alliances have weakened, our friends have become ambivalent, and our enemies emboldened.

At home, by deeply (and perhaps disastrously) dividing the nation into those "who are with us" and those "who are against us" the President has polarized the country. Instead of being a symbol of national unity, he has fostered a condition of civil war.

Fear and Hope

Bolshevism teaches that in order to control the masses the leader should instill fear and hope.

The President expressed plenty of hope in the "Audacity of Hope" and has been peddling plenty of fear in his speeches and actions. Fear-mongering, intimidation, dema-goguery and lies are a potent weapon of regimes having a hidden agenda. For the Obama administration and the liberal democrats who are dreaming of converting the USA, the United States of America into the USSA, the United Socialist States of America, all means are acceptable to accomplish this historic (in their minds) objective.

The President has been frightening this country by manufacturing threats from such Obama-declared enemies as Wall Street, the undue influence of big corporations, special interest groups, and the so-called extremists of the Tea Party. Obama did not hesitate to publicly intimidate the Supreme Court to secure a favorable outcome for the so-called Obama Care legislation.

The President is using scare tactics constantly to support his agenda. Remember the banks bailout? Obama warned: if we do not bail out the banks, the economy will collapse; if there is no stimulus package, unemployment will be above 8%; if we do not bail out GM and Chrysler, the automobile industry will cease to exist. We were told the economy would sink into a deep recession if the "Jobs Bill" was not approved by Congress and money was not handed out to "too-big-to-fail" corporate cronies and so on. The list goes on: If the debt ceiling is not increased then Social Security Retirees, Military Retirees, Social Security disability, and Federal Retirees will not get their govern-ment checks.

"Scaring the American people is exactly what President Obama is doing," Sarah Palin said. "The President is getting pretty good at this fear mongering and trying to cram down the public's throat this idea of bigger government, more spending."

As with all followers of Marxism-Leninism, the President fanatically believes in his own righteousness and superior intellect. His Bolshevik arrogance and exuberant confidence in his ability to change the country, commingled with disrespect and contempt for the outgoing administration and personally for President Bush, was in full display during his inauguration.

However, faced with the reality of governing, Obama has attempted to camouflage his lack of leadership with passionate speeches, but his passion and eloquence can only obscure reality; it cannot change it. There is not a shred of evidence that any of the calamities that he is predicting will ever occur. There is no evidence that the "Jobs Bill" would ever stimulate the economy and produce a meaningful reduction in unemployment; actually, there is evidence that points to the contrary. Furthermore, the President and Democrats know that their exuberant promises cannot be fulfilled. Given the existing regulations and constraints imposed by Obama's EPA, just getting permits for a substantial infrastructure project will take years. However, all of Obama's threats and all his proposed legislation, have one common remedy: spending more money.

Effluence and Affluence

Conventional wisdom would say that in order to get reelected, the President should get off his socialist donkey and offer a comprehensive economic plan that would get the support of both Republicans and Democrats. However, as I stated earlier the President does not follow conventional wisdom. He is following the Bolsheviks' ideology that great ideas can be realized in one grand ideological assault.

Wrapping himself in a cloak of morality, the President is skillfully transforming the socialist effluence into political affluence. He insists that the unequal distribution of wealth is a major ethical issue before the American people. In his State of the Union address the President called it:

> *"The defining issue of our time". "No challenge is more urgent. No debate is more important,"* the President declared.

This statement in the State of the Union address declares the President's strategic imperative. It validates the President's priorities and explains the lack of progress on other "minor" issues of our time like the national debt, high unemployment, and economic stagnation. The President has admitted in unambiguous terms that his objectives have nothing to do with the economy, stupid. The economy simply is not "the defining issue of our time." Got it?

It is becoming remarkably evident that Obama is attempting to frame the terms of the debate away from the state of the economy. The Democrats like to talk about gay marriage, contraceptives, inequality, anything but the economy and the national debt. It may be shrewd politics, but the President is having a difficult time hiding his true agenda from the American people.

Although he is relentlessly trying to convey his concerns about the economy, Obama's message is increasingly confusing. The President, by his own words, is confirming my earlier assertion that the economy is not his top priority. What exactly is the President telling the nation? What are his priorities? Is it getting the country out of the recession or manufacturing socialism? The more the American people try to digest it, the more mystifying and contradictory it appears.

"We've got to choose which direction we want this country to go," Obama said. "Do we want to keep giving those tax breaks to folks like me who don't need them? Or do we want to keep investing in those things that keep our economy growing and keep us secure? That's the choice." Hence, tax reductions are bad for the economy. Right? Not so fast.

It seems that the President made this choice earlier when he said, "The last thing you want to do is raise taxes in the middle of the recession because that would just suck up and take more demand out of the economy and put businesses in a further hole." Hence, raising taxes is also bad for the economy.

Moreover, the President's $447 billion Jobs Bill before Congress contains $245 billion worth of payroll tax cuts in order to stimulate the economy. Hence, tax reductions are good for the economy. Are we making any sense here? Which one is it, Mr. President?

Do dollars from the middle class stimulate the economy but dollars from the rich do not? Are the dollars from the middle class greener than the dollars from the rich? Is the President making any sense here? Help me: I need a Tylenol.

Obamamism

Switching gears, Obama also told students at Florida Atlantic University that "what drags our entire economy down" is when "the gap between those at the very, very top and everybody else keeps growing wider and wider and wider and wider." Never mind that since Marx's "Das Kapital" saw the light of day 150 years ago, there has been no shred of evidence to suggest that income disparity has anything to do with economic growth.

The President has invented a new economic theory—let's call it Obamamism, which Karl Marx would undoubtedly appreciate. According to the President, in order to get the economy going we have to close the gap—take from the rich and give to everybody else. It is that simple. Unfortunately, Obama's historical memories do not include the lessons of his Soviet ideological predecessors. How did this simple formula work out for them? The answer is now a matter of history.

To substantiate his argument the President is resurrecting an old Karl Marx theory, of "relative poverty." Karl Marx, unable to deny the obvious—that capitalism offers upward mobility for all segments of the population —developed a theory of relative poverty. The purpose of the theory was to substantiate Marx's concept of capitalist exploitation of working people. The essence of the theory is that, although the overall society is getting richer, the rich people accumulate wealth faster that people in lower income brackets. Therefore, working people are not getting their fair share of prosperity. And, with time, people in lower income brackets, despite their income growing, are getting poorer and poorer. Relatively speaking, of course.

Although, this phenomenon has been evident to everyone since the Greeks invented mathematics, the Left has enthusiastically embraced it and used income disparity as a propaganda tool against the capitalist system.

For those few of us who never went to school or, perhaps, are having a senior moment, consider this: If you have a million dollars invested at a 10% yearly return, at the end of the year you get $100,000. However, if you have only invested $100,000, you get only ten thousand dollars. That is a simple explanation for income disparity. Clearly, it is good to be rich—that is why we all aspire to shoot for the moon. As my teacher told me, even if you miss, you will still land among the stars. But the President's vision for America is to bring us down into the socialist gutter.

The President, unable or unwilling to decipher the truth from spin, is prepared to say anything, no matter how ridiculous it sounds, just to distract the country's attention from his real objectives.

More Power to the Poor

One thing is becoming exceedingly evident. Obama has been very passionate about raising taxes on the rich, regardless of its impact on the economy. Why? He has never articulated whether he feels it is necessary on economic grounds, as a road to prosperity; or on moral grounds, as a road to socialist virtue?

"We cannot afford $1 trillion worth of tax cuts for every millionaire and billionaire in our society. We can't afford it. And I refuse to renew them again. In the end, that's what this election is about. Do we participate in a politics of cynicism or a politics of hope?" The President declared. I would hope neither. We have not elected a spiritual leader to offer us hope. Hope is neither a plan, nor a strategy, nor a solution. We have elected the President to provide leadership, to offer a coherent strategy for getting our country out of an economic slump and to project a vision for the future.

If raising taxes is an economic issue and the purpose of raising taxes is a reduction of the deficit, as the President and his supporters are implying, it will not work. The proposed tax increase on the rich would raise around seventy billion dollars per year. Considering we have a one trillion dollar annual shortfall, it is minuscule in comparison with the deficit, making it irrelevant.

As we should have learned from experience, there is no correlation between the taxes we pay and the money we spend. Every time the administration tells us that taxes will pay for the deficit, it never happens. When Ronald Reagan took office the deficit was $1.0 trillion. Taxes were raised a number of times since; the current deficit is $16 trillion. Furthermore, when the President said that raising taxes during a recession would put businesses in a further hole, he made it clear that raising taxes is not an economic issue. Hence, we have to assume it is a moral issue.

Without challenging the morality of raising taxes, we can all agree with the President that raising taxes during a recession is the wrong approach. Then, it is fair to ask: Why is the President prepared to risk an economic downturn and why is he spending so much of his time and political capital on this incendiary issue, particularly if there is no imperative to seek its resolution as long as the economy is in a recession? The President may be better served raising taxes once we are out of the recession; it certainly would increase his credibility and eliminate the argument that doing so sucks money out of the economy.

Perhaps it is difficult to the untrained eye to see the logic and purpose of this presidential gambit. However, if the American people could wear my magic red communist glasses they would see a clear picture of the President's well-coordinated efforts summarized in the following two quotes:

"This is the moment when we must build on the wealth that open markets have created, and share its benefits more equitably." And, *"I think when you spread the wealth around, it's good for everybody."*

We do not know how it could be good for those whose wealth will be spread around. What's more we have no idea who will be on the receiving end of this generosity. The President did not elaborate any further, but I will:

Being a Marxist, the President believes that wealth is produced by the exploitation of the working class. Therefore, it must be redeemed back to society as a form of taxes and welfare.

Obama's actions confirm, once again, what we knew from the start: that the economy, the deficit, and unemployment are just a smog screen to divert the country's attention from his main and only objective, which he is prepared to implement at any cost.

The President is not interested in economic growth, prosperity and other attributes of a capitalist society; he is interested in ambiguity and poverty.

Ambiguity allows Obama to demonstrate that he is working hard to solve the nation's problems and fighting the enemies sabotaging the government's efforts to protect the middle class, and save social security etc. Maintaining poverty ensures dependency and provides the votes to fashion the perception of legitimacy.

"In a democracy the poor will have more power than the rich, because there are more of them, and the will of the majority is supreme."

Aristotle (Ancient Greek Philosopher, Scientist *and* Physician, *384 BC-322 BC*)

And, to get reelected, President Obama needs more of them.

Who is Rich? Not Me.

As we said earlier, contrary to prevailing wisdom, class warfare or class struggle as Lenin called it, does work. The philosophy of envy and siphoning from the rich appeals to a large segment of the population that does not realize that the definition of "the rich" is a spiral of devolution that eventually will reach every business and every individual that works for a living.

I watched pollster Frank Luntz the other day on FOX. In front of a room full of people, Luntz tried to define the fair tax rate for the rich. Luntz started asking people, "What do you think is fair? Is 90%? Let's say I make $10,000,000. Would it be fair if I paid 90%?"

One lady said, "Of course, you can live pretty well on $1,000,000."

So then he asked, "What is your household income?"

She said, "About two hundred thousand dollars." I am sure that a person who makes $50,000 a year, thinks $200,000 is a fortune; and that she could probably live just fine on $100,000—why not tax her at 50%. The point is that someone making less is not the best authority on how someone wealthier should spend their money, or be taxed.

It is easy to be fair with other people's money. This woman obviously never had $10 Million, so she treats it like a lottery ticket. But for someone who made it, the money represents this person's sweat and blood, sleepless nights and the torture of failure. It is an agony of responsibility for employees, their mortgages, private schools and retirement. That money is meant to replace outdated equipment and, is also a cushion to weather downturns. And, most importantly, it is his or her money. I remember the advice I got from a Lebanese businessman a long time ago, "you will never get rich counting other people's money."

Now, the reason that taxing the rich has not been legislated by Congress yet, is that they can't agree who is "The Rich." I know the answer: "The Rich" is "everyone who lives better than me." Isn't that simple? I hope that, eventually, Congress agrees with me.

The Voting Herd

In order to continue spending, the President must put pressure on the Republicans in the House and Congress. As far as the Democrats are concerned, they have never met a spending proposal they didn't like. During the last thirty years the Democratic Party has evolved, in effect, into the Social Democratic Party. Whether the leadership and membership realize it or not, the Democratic Party has been proliferating socialism in this country by "giving Americans small doses of socialism" just as Khrushchev predicted back in 1959 during a meeting with then secretary of agriculture Ezra Benson. The socialist venom has accumulated in the American organism and eventually poisoned the Democratic Party. No wonder that the President enjoys the full and unequivocal support of the Democratic Party for his socialist agenda.

The Democrats do not debate Obama's legislative proposals or question his agenda; they support unequivocally and unanimously every Presidential initiative without even reading them before voting. Remember the infamous words of former Speaker of the House Nancy Pelosi that, "We have to pass the [health care] bill so that you can find out what is in it."

Their devotion to the President and the socialist cause has turned the Democrats in the House and Senate into what the Bolshevik Leon Trotsky called the *"Voting herd,"* acting much like the Soviet Congress of People's Representatives that for seventy years always unanimously approved the Communist party's programs. The interests of the public, the wellbeing of the country, the state of the economy, and future of this nation are taking a back seat to the interests of the Party and President.

What is most troubling is that even responsible democrats like Bill Clinton support Obama's agenda. Does President Clinton now believe that he was wrong when he reduced government spending to the lowest level in three decades, or when he enacted comprehensive welfare reform, or achieved the largest deficit reduction in history, or cut the federal bureaucracy by more than 100,000 positions and reduced the White House staff by 25 percent?

Clinton was not wrong; he has just surrendered his prestige and principles for political expediency, thereby evidencing the moral bankruptcy of the Democratic Party. Clinton missed the opportunity to act as a statesman and, in this critical moment for the country, do the right thing and make history. Incredibly, unembarrassed by his new-found convictions, Clinton is allying himself with the radical left serving Obama to dismantle Clinton's own legacy. There is something intrinsically wrong within the Democratic Party.

There is no question that Clinton's position is not substantive, but rather cynical. The rank and file Democrats who voted for Clinton reflect this metamorphosis. They support the party without regard to the issues. Their unequivocal support of Obama's vision for America is so diametrically opposed to Clinton's legacy that it only confirms this contention. The Democrats are voting the party line, using Nancy Pelosi's mentality: vote for our candidate so that we can find out how he or she is going to change our country.

It is almost inconceivable that, in just twelve years, the Democrats have moved from conditional support of Clinton to unconditional support of Obama, which con-stitutes a complete reversal of their values and vision for the country. What drove this democratic liberalism into outright war on American values was the emergence of radicalism in the Democratic Party that has more to do with Marxism and Leninism than with democratic principles.

It is obvious that the Democratic Party has changed in the last 20 years. Calling themselves democrats is a misnomer because they do not represent the party of John F. Kennedy, Daniel Patrick Moynihan or Bill Clinton for that matter.

In its ideological conversion, the party moved way to the far left and as part of this process, they packed Marx's "Das Kapital" and Lenin's "What Is to Be Done?" in their briefcases. The change in values was on full display during Obama's inauguration.

The ostentatious inauguration of duly elected president Barack Obama, emulating the inauguration of Gaius Julius Caesar including a recreation of the Tempio del Divo Giulio in Rome, was not seen by Democrats as offensive or distasteful. Nor did they find the price tag of $150 million dollars spent on the inauguration festivities, cynical and insulting to the millions of unemployed Americans.

The Democrats are not embarrassed by the exclusive and lavish lifestyle of the President and First Lady. While Americans suffer high unemployment and a rising cost of living, the American royal family travels in style taking super-luxury vacations all over the world, including taking the kids to London for fish and chips on the taxpayer's dime. The First Family lifestyle is reminiscent of African dictators and Arab sheiks. The First Lady alone is enjoying her unprecedented staff of twenty-two servants at a cost of $1.5 million per year.

What a startling contrast to fellow Democratic president Harry Truman. As President, Truman paid for all of his own travel expenses and food. When offered corporate positions at large salaries, he declined, stating, "You don't want me. You want the office of the President, and that doesn't belong to me. It belongs to the American people and it's not for sale."

Today, politicians have found a way to cash in and become quite wealthy while enjoying the fruits of their offices. Good old Harry Truman was correct when he observed, "My choices early in life were either to be a piano player in a whore house or a politician. And to tell the truth, there's hardly any difference."

As Baron Acton said 150 or so years ago, "Power tends to corrupt, and absolute power corrupts absolutely." The Democrats, while in control of the House and Senate, have brought corruption to a new shameless level as Representatives were openly accepting bribes to vote for the Health Care Bill.

Senator Ben Nelson, Democrat of Nebraska, who voted for the bill, not only accepted a bribe to vote for it but nevertheless requested a waiver for his state. So, if this bill is good for the country, why not for Nebraska? Conversely, if it is not good for the people of Nebraska, why is it good for the rest of the country?

The so-called "Louisiana purchase" is another example. Sen. Mary Landrieu bargained $300 million for her vote, camouflaged as government assistance to Katrina victims. The list of the bribed is so long that it would take a chapter to list them all.

It was refreshing to see the Republicans demonstrating Republican incorruptibility. No Republican accepted a bribe and not for the lack of persuasion.

The integrity of the Senate Democrats, or rather the lack of it, was tested in 2008 when Illinois Governor Rod Blagojevich was poised to make a Senate appointment to replace the seat of President-Elect Barack Obama as junior senator from Illinois. "Senate Democrats made it clear weeks ago that they cannot accept an appointment made by a governor who is accused of selling this very Senate seat. I agree with their decision," President-Elect Obama said.

Blagojevich, however, made a capping play with a knight's move; he appointed his friend Roland Wallace Burris, who happened to be black, to the Senate seat. The President immediately accepted it.

The reaction of the President and the Democratic Senate mirrors the story of Roman emperor Caligula who once made his favorite horse a senator. It seems as if, had Blagojevich appointed a horse to the United States Senate, the President and Senators would support it, as long as it was...... a black horse, of course.

The Bolshevik Strategy

American Idealism and pluralism, that have been a

foundation for this country since its inception, are being replaced with a set of morals foreign to American values.

In order to succeed, as the Bolsheviks' teaching goes, the government needs to take control of the economy and dominate everyday life by making its citizens dependent on the government. The Bolsheviks' promise of a social paradise was a lure to make Russia's citizens dependent on government handouts. To accomplish this Lenin said, *"Debauch the currency to overturn the basis of society."* The Bolsheviks created hyper-inflation to make the currency, the Russian ruble, worthless—thereby destroying personal wealth. Their gambit succeeded: Russia's economy was paralyzed and the Bolshevik government was able to solidify their control over all aspects of their citizens' life.

"They don't get us! They don't get who we are!" yelled Joe Biden before the crowd of supporters.

Oh, yes, Mr. Vice President, we know who you are.

Obama's long-term strategy for the implementation of the socialist dream can be elucidated based on a preponderance of the evidence and the application of the theories of Marxism and Leninism. In his quest to re-engineer the free market economy and replace American self-reliance with government dependency, the President is using methods developed by the Russian Bolsheviks during the early stages of the Bolshevik revolution in Russia. His strategy rests on three pillars, which are fundamentally interrelated and interdependent:

1. Destruction of Wealth

Obama is clearly following Lenin's strategy for the downfall of capitalism, spending and printing money at unprecedented levels. Be it for bailouts, stimulus plans, health care, manure management, tattoo removal, condoms, or solar energy, whatever the program—the area doesn't really matter. I suspect that some of you think that I was using hyperbole to make a dramatic statement. Regrettably, it was no exaggeration; it is all too true. The Stimulus Bill does include: $200,000 for tattoo removal, $335 million for condoms and sexually explicit "STD prevention" programs and, thanks to the courtesy of Tom Harkin, almost $2 million for swine odor and manure management.

What is really dramatic, is the growth of the country's national debt during the last three years. From 1977 up to the end of President Bush's term in 2008, the debt reached $ 10.6 trillion. During the Obama presidency, the debt has grown by more than 60% and has now reached $16 trillion which amounts to nearly 100% of the projected Gross Domestic Product and the President wants to spend even more.

Nothing is going to stop this President from spending our money. His administration demonstrates a high level of creativity when it comes to spending. The newest ideas are a "jobs bank" with a 1.5 billion budget, relaxing student loan repayment rules to allow many students not to repay their loans, very generous foreign aid, and even advertisements to recruit Welfare recipients.

The government is running up mountains of debt with increasing speed. The Great spender, G.W. Bush, looks like a fiscally responsible president compared to Obama.

It is becoming exceedingly evident that the President's objective is to spend until the country is in such debt as to result in a state of hyper-inflation that causes the destruction of our currency. The US government will then flood the markets with cheap dollars devaluating the net worth of productive citizens and successful enterprises, and, in this manner, enable the obliteration of wealth.

This explains why this President and his Democratic allies in Congress have not passed a budget in the last four years. The budget is a controlling document designed to identify and manage expenditure. If there is no budget, there are no restrictions on spending; the gates are wide open. The issue here is not whether we are talking about a Republican proposed budget or the Democratic budget; "no budget" is the only acceptable option for this President. By law the President of the United States must propose a budget and the legislature's job is to debate, amend, and pass it. The President proposed a budget so ridiculous that even his Democratic voting herd rejected it. The Senate vote on the Presidential budget was 99 to 0 against it.

The Republicans in the House did not wait for the President to offer leadership on the issue; they passed Paul Ryan's budget and sent it to the Senate. The President and

Democrats then attacked the budget like a pack of sharks sensing blood. The media unmercifully denounced the budget as radical and ideological. It exercised its prerogative in selecting the data that supports their ideological preference.

Despite all the criticism and ridicule of the Republican budget, Harry Reid, the Senate Majority Leader, refused to bring it to the floor for a vote. Why? Because the "voting herd" after the 2010 Congressional elections got the message and was not as coherent as it was in 2008. There was a distinct possibility that some renegades may cross the ideological barricade and work with the Republicans to develop a pragmatic and realistic approach to the budget that both sides could vote for. The President and Harry Reid could not take that risk.

So, instead, here's how it goes: the government spends and later requests raising the debt ceiling so it can borrow more. The Congress, facing the US Government default on its obligations, has no other option but to approve additional borrowing because the money has already been spent. And so it goes, with the national debt now reaching 16 trillion dollars and, given that it is rising by the second, by the time this book is out it could be a lot more.

When Republican Presidential candidate Rick Perry accused the chairman of the Federal Reserve Ben S. Bernanke of treachery for unrestrained printing of US Dollars, the press loudly condemned him. But Perry was literally right on the money for accusing the Chairman of undermining the US currency and the stability of the country's economic system. It would be impossible to assume that the Chairman, who is a Nobel Laureate in economics, did not understand the ramifications of his actions. It is also hard to believe that the Chairman and the President did not realize that the combination of increasing deficit and a flood of American dollars would lead to inflation and the de facto devaluation of the currency.

Any time the Fed inflates the money supply it steals buying power from people who hold dollar denominated accounts including retiree savings and pensions. Stealing under any other circumstances would be criminal. But since the government is doing it, I doubt that Obama's Attorney General Eric Holder will take the case.

In personal terms, if you have $500,000 in your 401K, or savings account, or US Treasury bills you may have been looking forward to an independent and relatively secure retirement. But if the currency is devaluated, let's say ten to one, and then you have only $50,000 of purchasing power —you will have to seek government assistance. Henry Ford once said, "Money makes a man free." By contrast, the more money the government takes from its citizens, the less freedom they have. This process, already underway by the Obama administration, shall continue until the complete submission of the nation.

2. Replacing American Self-reliance with Government Dependency

The President and his allies understand that getting

Americans to accept socialism is like putting a saddle on a cow. It would require a major moral adjustment in Americans' DNA—replacement of American self-reliance with government dependency.

Dependency plays a major role in the President's strategy of fundamentally changing America; independence to be replaced with obedience, self-reliance with submissiveness, and eventually submissiveness will lead to bondage. The more American people are indebted to the government, the more they will turn to the government to save them, assuring Democratic one-party rule for the future. The President is not far from achieving his objective, considering how much this country has changed since its inception.

Although Obama lost the Congress, he still has the power of the Executive office and the Federal Reserve to print more dollars until they become worthless. So, if anyone thinks that our journey to socialism has stopped, I would suggest, think again. It did suffer a setback with the 2010 mid-term elections, but the train is still moving.

When I wrote the first in my series of articles, "Anatomy of a Bolshevik," in November 2010, 47% of Americans did not pay any income tax. Recently, the Heritage Foundation estimated that 51% of Americans are not paying any income tax, and the number is growing.

According to government statistics, more than 30 million Americans are getting welfare checks, 44 million are receiving food stamps, 8 million are getting SSI (Social Supplementary Income), and millions enjoy subsidized housing. It may be an eye opener for some of us that a vast number of Americans are already living in virtual communism, receiving government handouts, in one form or another, "in accordance with their needs." This new debased class of citizens—freeloaders whose whole existence is contingent upon government generosity constantly demands more and more largess from their masters. Obama is not going to disappoint his most dependent and dependable constituency.

More goodies in the administration pipeline include free health care, free tuition, more welfare, contraception pills, seemingly inexhaustible unemployment benefits, subsidized mortgages; and the list goes on and on.

Obama knows exactly how agreeably his promises fall on the ears of freeloaders who have been conditioned for decades to support the Democrats through increased financial dependency. What do you think Obama bought with the additional five trillion dollars of debt we accumulated during the first term of his presidency? A better economy? Better schools? A safer environment? No, he bought more dependency. More government employees, more police officers, more teachers, more food stamps, more welfare; all these people in one way or other depend on the government.

A recent report by Diane Sawyer of ABC offers more evidence about the President's priorities. Sawyer reported about government financed infrastructure projects in New York, Alaska, and California with a total price tag around $7.8 billion that were awarded to Chinese construction firms, despite a high level of unemployment in the U.S. construction industry. Why???

Because this administration values dependency over employment.

I am intimately familiar with the side effects of dependency. The Soviet system was built on dependency. Dependency is a chronic disease that is difficult to cure. As Karl Marx observed, "social existence determines consciousness." Many of those who stay on welfare or other government programs lose, over time, the capacity to be productive. All they have is a delusion that it's the government's obligation to provide support for the less fortunate. It is not, after all, their fault; it is just a matter of misfortune.

When I look at my two beautiful cats, I see a parallel between them and this huge and ever-expanding segment of American society. Many hundreds, perhaps thousands, of years ago, the ancestors of my cats lived in the wilderness and provided for themselves and their offspring. But over time, they became domesticated and totally dependent on humans. They lost the capacity to hunt, to defend themselves from enemies, and to survive on their own. If one day I decided to throw them out on the street, they would die from starvation and disease. That is what dependency does to people—they became socialists.

Another way for the present administration to extend their dominion is to widen the membership of government-friendly trade unions by solidifying the union bosses' control over the rank and file. This is exactly the plan behind the "Employee Free Choice Act"—legislation that deprives workers of free choice by replacing private balloting with publicly signed cards in the presence of union bosses. It is not a new invention, like most of the President's ideas, this one has been borrowed from the Kremlin's revolutionary library. The Bolsheviks called it, "The Principle of Democratic Centralism." So-called "Democratic Centralism" had nothing to do with democracy and everything to do with subjugation and control of the labor movement by making it an extension of the Communist Party. In this country the administration would love nothing more than to use a forced expansion of labor unions as a vehicle to gain extraordinary powers and a reliable source of election financing.

The Universal Health Care Bill is the key to the President and his allies' agenda of putting the harness collar of socialism on the neck of the American people.

We can all agree that the existing health system is a disgrace, to put it mildly. Critics point out the high cost, lack of transferability in case of an employer-provided option, pre-existing conditions that cause people to lose insurance when they lose employment or change jobs, and that millions of people don't have access to health care, among many other issues. It is not the purpose of this book to debate these issues, nor offer any solution to the problem. I will leave that to others. However, what I do want to point out, is the way in which the President makes political use of this issue. In actuality, the President is not interested in solving the problem. He just does not want this crisis to go to waste.

The Health Care bill is a cornerstone in the President's bid to restructure American society. The American Neo-Bolsheviks spent two years exploiting a crisis to advance a socialist agenda using the full range of their potent weapons from demagoguery and lies, distortion, misrepresentation, and intimidation to common bribery to push the law down the throat of the American people.

The President's quotes below show the depth of deception and length the President and his allies were willing to go to achieve their objectives. Obama insisted that, "And so our goal on health care is, if we can get, instead of health care costs going up 6 percent a year, it's going up at the level of inflation, maybe just slightly above inflation, we've made huge progress. And by the way, that is the single most important thing we *could do in terms of reducing our deficit*. That's why we did it".

Later when the disparity between what the President says and what he does became all too obvious, the President was forced to admit the truth, "But if you—if what—the reports are true, what they're saying is, is that as a consequence of us getting 30 million additional people health care, at the margins that's going to increase our costs, *we knew that.*"

Of course he knew that. Suffice to say, that anyone who has a brain a little larger than a Neanderthal's should understand that extending health care to an additional 30 million people cannot cost less, and therefore cannot be "the single most important thing" we could do in terms of reducing the deficit. He knew that but continued to deliberately and repeatedly mislead the American people. Perhaps the President thought that the American people are ignorant fools. If so, he has a point here, they elected him.

After the legislation is fully implemented the government will have control over 17% of the American economy. This will create a new enormous bureaucracy that will regulate and dictate how health care is delivered; who can provide it, to whom it is provided, at what cost, what medical devices and procedures can be used etc. They will even have access to the individuals' bank accounts to ensure universal purchase of insurance.

It is difficult to estimate the total bill for his agenda but health care alone will cost this country $1.76 trillion dollars over the next ten years according to the CBO (The Congressional Budget Office), which has been notorious in underestimating almost any expenditure by the Federal Government. The Health Care bill is also recognized as a major contributor to the deficit. The main reason for the cost is that households with incomes below 400% and above 133% of the federal poverty line (FPL) who are enrolled in insurance plans are eligible for premium assistance financed by the federal government. In other words, millions of people will get it for free, or so they were led to believe.

No one described the enticement of getting something for free as well as the great Russian writer Mikhail Bulgakov. In his famous novel "The Master and Margarita," to depict the soul of socialism, he described Satan's visit to Moscow. During a show that Lucifer has arranged at a local theatre, the audience is showered with banknotes falling from the ceiling. People start fighting each other to catch the money. Then Satan makes a clothing store appear on stage and people are invited to change their old clothes for luxurious outfits. Again, a brawl erupts but the winners look like they just came from a Paris fashion show. Satan watches the crowd, amused, saying, "For the last 2000 years they haven't changed a bit." As soon as the show ends, the money turns to useless paper and the luxurious clothes disappear, leaving the "lucky" people completely naked.

3. The Replacement of a Capitalist Market-oriented Economy with a Government-controlled Political Economy

As Karl Marx advised, "The way to crush the bourgeoisie (read: capitalism) is to grind them between the millstones of taxation and inflation." Obama has taken it a step further, adding to the millstones of taxation and inflation a huge national debt, the high cost of energy, and an enormous expansion of the Federal Government. He has also imposed additional government regulations that greatly impair the ability of business to expand and innovate.

Just as any living organism needs oxygen and water to

sustain life, the capitalist economy needs capital and cheap energy to thrive. Therefore, it is not a coincidence that the financial and energy sectors became targets for new regulations. Respectively, the Dodd-Frank Wall Street Reform and Consumer Protection Act and the Cap & Trade Bill are each imposing much stricter regulations on these sectors, making them further dependent on government regulators.

According to the government, the Dodd-Frank Wall Street Reform and Consumer Protection bill is designed to address the increasing propensity of the financial sector to put the entire system at so great a risk that it eventually needs to be bailed out at taxpayer's expense. In plain English it is supposed to take the risk out of the banking business. Talk about a contradiction in terms!

This Act brought the most significant changes to financial regulation in the United States since the regulatory reform that followed the Great Depression. This act, however, will not prevent another financial crisis or additional "bail-outs" of financial institutions, much as its proponents would like us to believe. As we know, the government has been enacting new laws and regulations after each economic and financial meltdown for the last two hundred years. The outcome of this latest one has already been felt by businesses and consumers. It unduly restricts the ability of banks and other financial institutions to make loans.

Dodd-Frank has created yet another huge bureaucracy to regulate the financial sector of the US economy. The Act rests on the assertion that government bureaucrats understand the financial sector better than the captains of the financial industry. The absurdity of this assertion was demonstrated by the President himself after the announcement that JP Morgan lost two billion dollars on a risky trade.

President Obama called the JP Morgan CEO Jamie Dimon "one of the smartest bankers we have got" and praised JPMorgan as "one of the best managed banks there is." What could government bureaucrats possibly know that CEO Jamie Dimon, one of smartest bankers in the universe, and his executives do not?

The President and the Democrats that fought to pass the bill as a supreme "savoir faire" should be embarrassed to see how the bill has failed in its first encounter with the reality of marketplace.

For Obama the bill does what it is supposed to do—greatly enhance the power of government regulators over the banking industry.

"You do not have some inherent right just to get a certain amount of profit if your customers are being mistreated," President Obama said, explaining the creation of a new government agency, the Consumer Financial Protection Bureau (CFPB). This new bureau has been granted enormous power to decide not only whether banks have the right to make a profit but also how much if someone, somewhere, was allegedly mistreated. In the real world, it is designed to restrict profits. No due process is required.

The energy sector will not fare any better under The Cap and Trade bill.

The Cap and Trade bill is otherwise known as the American Clean Energy and Security Act. The bill seeks to impose significant limits on the amount of greenhouse gases that energy producers and manufacturers can emit into the atmosphere each year. According to its proponents, the bill is designed to curb Global Warming and promote alternative energy production. In reality, it is a tax on US energy producers and end users, for the purpose of raising the cost of conventional sources of electricity, thereby making alternative energies competitive. It can also be used as an instrument of political pressure. As with any regulation enacted by this administration, some entities will be granted exceptions to the rules. Plans are in the works to include some form of rebates in water and power bills to offset the higher cost of green power. Who gets those rebates will be politically determined.

To no one's surprise, in California where the program has been enacted, it has become a giant government program to socialize the extraordinarily high rates of electricity, natural gas, and water bills.

As is usually the case with a political economy, there have been unintended consequences. The President is caught in conflicting currents. The bill will raise the cost of electricity, and subsequently will have a negative impact on the President's dream to replace internal combustion engines with electric cars. It will certainly raise unemployment in such states as Pennsylvania and Virginia; and coal miners will not be happy in this election year. Furthermore, the higher cost of energy will be reflected in every manufactured good, from food to airplanes, and, as a result, more businesses will choose to move overseas. Even these reasons will not stop Obama from enacting his agenda to reduce American dependence on oil.

The President's efforts to power the 16-trillion-dollar economy with windmills and solar panels have proved to be a colossal fiasco. His latest proposal, to manufacture fuel from algae, though a far cry from the discovery of electricity or the invention of the internal combustion engine is a vast improvement over his earlier proposal to reduce American oil usage by inflating tires and tuning up engines.

One may ask, "Why are we continuing to play in Obama's theater of the absurd?" Primarily, because the President is taking control of the economy and is favoring industries that cannot survive without government assistance. Secondly, in his need to be admired and in his aspiration to greatness, he is trying to elicit the adulation of his key supporters: the Left as well as the environmental fanatics who would like to send this civilization back to the Bronze Age.

Nothing Tangible

The country is undergoing a period of upheaval. Unfortunately, the Philosopher President has neither the experience nor the inclination to lead a national debate about the future of this country. Especially, when the future he envisions, reminiscent of Greece and other Western European countries or even the Soviet Union, runs contrary to American Idealism and values.

When business owners and CEOs complain that the Obama administration is the most anti-business administration in American history, they need to understand that this President's agenda is not about business, it is about social justice; it is not about wealth creation, it is about wealth redistribution; it is not about law, it is about fairness; it is not about individualism, it is about collectivism; it is not about self-reliance, it is about dependency, and finally, whether they like it or not; it is not about capitalism, it is about socialism.

The President has an agenda but he has no program to sell to the nation. When it comes to the economy, energy, emigration, environment, foreign policy or any other substantive issue, the President lacks coherent operational policy. Yet, on each issue, Obama skillfully transforms liability into benefit. He offers ambiguous slogans and undefined objectives.

Lack of direction leads to desperation and desperation leads to a continuation of national crises. Demagogues thrive in this type of environment. Perhaps future historians will have various explanations for the Presidential disconnect between saying and doing, however, as I see it through my communist glasses, it resembles communist practice at its worst. I am compelled to quote Lenin again, "To rely upon conviction, devotion, and other excellent spiritual qualities; that are not to be taken seriously in politics." The President wants to be taken seriously. Thus, when the President makes a promise we should expect exactly the opposite:

If the President talks about reduction of the deficit we should expect the deficit to rise.

If the President talks about reducing the Federal Government, we should expect a bigger government.

If the President talks about cooperation, we should expect more confrontation.

If the President talks about reducing the cost of health care, we should expect the cost to go up.

If the President talks about energy independence, we should expect moratoriums on drilling.

If the President talks about reducing taxes, we should expect taxes to go up.

If the President talks about banks loaning more money, we should expect new rules that would prevent banks from loaning the money.

But if the President tells us that he wants to spread the wealth around, you better believe him!

In this environment, the President is selling emotions. He is making passionate speeches from a copy of the election-year play book telling the nation what needs to be done. But he would not tell us how. Hence, having nothing tangible to offer he is using his powers of locution to mobilize the constituency to accomplish his objectives through brute force, outmaneuvering his critics in the process.

Despite the fact that the President has refined his demagoguery into a high art reminiscent of Greek political oratory, the more he talks, the more he exposes his "Poverty of Philosophy."

Chapter Three

Who are you, Mr. President?

Tell me about Your Friends

Tell me about Your Friends

While in the Soviet Union, I was told that anyone in the United States could become President. I did not believe it. After the election of Barack Hussein Obama, I do believe it.

The 2008 elections resulted in what, to many people, was a totally unexpected state of political and economic affairs. The most fundamental factor was a misunderstanding, or a lack of understanding, of the future president's background, his philosophy, his convictions and the exact nature of the change that he so successfully promulgated during the campaign. His rhetoric lacked a conceptual description of his beliefs and convictions; nonetheless, the public bought it.

It was like during the Bolshevik revolution in Russia: People were excited; there was going to be democracy, freedom, liberty, land to peasants, bread to the hungry, power to the people—those Bolshevik slogans sounded great but were never meant to be. The Russian people expected the Great Change, but when it came, it was not what they expected.

Just like in Russia, where change was supported by the so called "intelligentsia," intellectuals who formed artistic, social, and/or political elite, in this country widely supported "Change" as did Hollywood, the media, and many wealthy individuals who shared Obama's socialist dreams.

For many people it was a time of rejoicing; America had made an incredible journey from the assassination of Martin Luther King Jr. to the inauguration of Barack Obama. In this state of political intoxication, they were not interested in the elected President's background and his political philosophy. What was important was that the President was black (even if his mother was white) and that he was a Democrat.

After four years in office, Obama still remains an enigma to the American people. The media imposed its version of a "don't-ask-don't-tell policy." They do not ask; and if some people do ask, then the media invokes racism, which is the Left's first line of defense when they cannot defend the merits of their position.

We know Obama attended Columbia and Harvard and earned a law degree. But we do not know what exactly he studied, how he managed to get accepted to those prestigious universities and how he paid for his education. Despite the fact that the President's employment, medical records and his tenure at Columbia and Harvard are sealed (I am sure for good reason) there has been no official inquiry to unseal the records.

Given the President's proclivity for self-promotion, if his academic accomplishments were something to write home about, the press would, no doubt, be elated to share facts about the President's intellectual capacities. The ease with which Obama moved from one prestigious university to another is another point of contention. After reading his biography "Dreams from My father" one gets the impression that the best universities in this country were competing to have Obama on their faculties. Why? Was he Albert Einstein? Or was it because of Affirmative Action or political correctness that compelled these universities to have a certain percentage of black students? We will never know the truth unless the President orders his files unsealed.

Although, I do not belong to the conspiracy theory crowd, I am troubled by the fact that Obama's birth was announced in two newspapers. Was it such a great event that it needed to be documented or was somebody trying to fabricate the evidence of his birth?

If there is a conspiracy, it is the press' refusal to investigate and inform the American public about the true nature of the President. This is all the more so, when it comes to the President's associations with former terrorists, American haters and common criminals. On this subject, with the exception of FOX news, the news media has been conspicuously silent.

For those with short memories, let me remind you that the President's associates includes Mr. Rezko, a real estate developer and major financial contributor when Obama ran for office in Chicago. Mr. Rezko has been convicted of fraud and bribery several times. On November 23, 2011, Rezko was sentenced to 10 1/2 years in prison.

Jeremiah Alvesta Wright, Jr., Obama's "spiritual mentor," is Pastor Emeritus of Trinity United Church of Christ (TUCC), in Chicago. Wright married Obama and his wife Michelle, baptized their two daughters. Wright is a notorious racist, anti-Semite, American-hater who has repeatedly denounced the U.S. Wright's sermons have even included the contention that the attacks of September 11, 2001, were proof that "America's chickens are coming home to roost" and such statements as "...not God Bless America. God damn America."

Bill Ayers and Bernardine Dohrn, long-time friends of Obama, are unrepentant terrorists, and former leaders of the 1960s' Weather Underground, America's first terrorist cult. They are responsible for a series of bombings including the Pentagon as well as bank robberies. The Weather Underground's goals were to establish "world communism" and "overthrow capitalism" and "imperialism" by any means necessary including "armed struggle."

Robert Malley, one of Obama's advisors, had regular contacts with the terrorist organization "Hamas."

Rashid Khalidi was Obama's friend and fundraiser. From 1972 through 1983, Khalidi was the director in Beirut of the official Palestinian press agency, FAFA. His wife worked there as well.

Then there is Frank Marshall Davis, a poet and member of the American Communist Party. From 1971 through 1979. While Obama was in Hawaii, the future president developed a close relationship with Davis, almost like father and son, listening to his poetry and getting indoctrination in Marxism.

Are you sick to your stomach yet?

"I chose my friends carefully. The more politically active black students. The foreign students. The Chicanos.

The Marxist professors and structural feminists and punk-rock performance poets."—Barack Obama wrote in "Dreams from My Father."

Well, what a coincidence that among Obama's Chicago neighbors were Larry Walsh, a criminal under investigation by the FBI; Louis Farrakhan, Leader of the Nation of Islam; and, of course his long-time friends, Bill Ayers and Bernardine Dohrn. What a distinguished neighborhood!

The defenders of the President call those accusations guilt by association. To which I say, *"Yes it is!"* Or as the Russians say, "Tell me about your friends and I can tell who you are."

I've heard the President's supporters argue that he was only eight years old when Bill Ayers committed his hideous crimes, therefore, they do not really see how it is related to the present. This is preposterous. I was not born when the Nazis committed their atrocities against the Jews, but would I invite a former Nazi to my house to have coffee? The fact that Bill Ayers donated $200 to Obama's Senate campaign and that the donation was accepted tells me that those two share more than coffee.

I would like my readers to ask themselves how many terrorists, former or current, they have personally met. Or if they have been dealing with a convicted criminal? Or would they continue their association with anyone who hates this country? I can go on and on. Yes, I do say the quality of your friends and associates does matter. Therefore, until we have a thorough, complete and independent investigation of all the facts surrounding Obama there will always be the temptation to judge the President by the quality of his associations, until proven otherwise.

By contrast, in the hallucinating eyes of the American media, Obama's past associations do not rise to the level of importance of Mitt Romney's alleged misbehaviors during his high school years. Thus the media did not cover Obama to the degree that many Americans may think he deserves.

The troubling thing is that a long list of American executives, experienced business people running major American corporations many of whom belong to the Fortune 500, supported Obama and donated money to his campaign. These people, who have splendid executive experience and substantial experience in hiring personnel for important positions, who would never hire a person with Obama's poor credentials and lack of experience for even a lowly management position in their company, nevertheless hired Obama to run this country—they voted for him. I feel for their embarrassment.

The reason I am confident that Obama would not be hired is because the man is woefully incompetent. The only logical explanation is that they were thinking that electing a black president would be the ultimate Affirmative Action.

I can hear voices of indignation on the Left defending the President's credentials. Webster Dictionary defines competence as having a sufficiency of means for subsistence, ability, adequacy and qualifications. I would also say the experience, track record of accomplishments and, finally, knowledge of the subject.

According to his autobiography "Dreams from My Father," Obama was hired after graduation by a consulting house (he would not tell us which), to a multinational corporation (he would not name), as a research assistant later promoted to the position of financial writer. According to him, he had an office, secretary and money in the bank. But after less than a year he was back in the street, broke, unemployed, eating soup from a can. He says, he decided to become a community organizer and started looking for an opportunity in organizing. He would not tell us against whom he was organizing and what the final objective was. We can only guess.

But nobody would hire him.

Eventually, a community organizer from Chicago, Marty Kaufman, saw potential in Obama and recruited him for his first organizing assignment. During the interview Kaufman got it right saying, "You must be angry about something." Kaufman then told him, "But not to worry. Anger is a prerequisite for the job. That is the only reason anybody decides to become an organizer." It makes one wonder what a young man who got the best education money could buy; who had launched a great career in corporate America, would be angry about. Just think about it.

During my years of emigration, I have met people who despised America and hated capitalism. They were convinced that an ordinary person cannot succeed in a society of "inequality and exploitation of working people." When these people find themselves on the verge of success, it destroys their convictions; they begin to see their own success as a personal defeat. They can't see themselves as gaining wealth and respect. They want to be victims.

Or perhaps, Obama just didn't want to get up in the morning and work. Perhaps, he was inspired by people like Jesse Jackson and Al Sharpton who were making a very good living organizing blacks and enjoyed notoriety. Or, perhaps he was simply fired for incompetence.

We will never know why Barack Obama decided to quit a respectable job and the paycheck that goes with it, to become a destitute community organizer. Any of the above versions are plausible. But regardless of the reason, his behavior exhibits the attributes of what Lenin called a professional revolutionary.

Given the President's associations and unimpressive employment record, we can say with a reasonable degree of certainty that a person of Obama's dubious credentials would never even get a government security clearance, yet he became the President of the United States.

Three years later, the same people who voted for him sound disappointed because they believed that Obama was a middle of the road politician. Really???? On what basis? Are we becoming so politically ignorant that failed to see the obvious? Have we lost our capacity to evaluate the facts? Are we taking our democracy for granted? Have we become complacent? Probably all of the above.

Consider the qualifications of some of our contemporary presidents; Jimmy Carter was a two term senator, and former governor; Dwight David "Ike" Eisenhower, was a five-star general, and Supreme Allied Commander; Richard Milhous Nixon, was a senator and two term Vice President; or Ronald Reagan, who was two time Governor of California; or George Herbert Walker Bush, the 41st President who was a two term Vice President, a congressman, ambassador and Director of the CIA, or take George Walker Bush, 43rd President, and Bill Clinton, both of whom were successful state governors. I could go on and on but I am sure you got my point.

Our President had limited experience as a community organizer, three terms as a State Senator and one uneventful term as a US Senator on his list of accomplishments.

It is difficult to ascertain how a man with no experience in anything, intellectually shallow with no record of accomplishment in anything, elevated himself into the Presidency of the United States?

Yes, I said "intellectually shallow" because passion and eloquence cannot be a substitute for substance. The President's public speeches about fairness and the alleged deficiencies of the capitalist system have never been translated into a sound economic or social policy.

This country has been confronted by serious economic and political challenges but the President, to no surprise, failed to preserve American leadership in defense of freedom and the proliferation of human rights. In the domestic arena, he has been incapable of offering a vision for the future, or of leading a national debate on the economy, foreign policy, immigration, entitlements, runaway spending, or any other substantive subject for that matter.

Nevertheless what Obama has accomplished is not just unprecedented it raises serious questions about our democratic process and even more so about us, the American people.

Dreams from his Father

In order to understand Obama we should look at his past for answers. Although we do not know much about the President we do know something from his autobiography and what the press was able to dig up.

During the 2008 elections Obama talked about dreams, about CHANGE, about a better America. What is Obama's American dream? He never elaborated about his dreams; he has never been specific about his vision for America.

In order to look into the President's soul we should be aware that he spent his youth, when most of us shape our character and values, outside of the United States. As far as we know, he lived in Indonesia, Pakistan and traveled frequently to Kenya.

Everyone views events through the prism of his own experience. In his autobiography, "Dreams from My Father" Obama implies that he dreams of implementing the dreams of his father. Yet the picture he paints of his father, Barack Obama, Sr., depicts a man that few, if any, would care to emulate. What could possibly his father had been dreaming of that so captivated his son? In his personal life, his father was a polygamist. He was married four times and had a habit of marrying one woman without bothering to divorce his current wife. He fathered eight children. Did his father dream of having a harem and fathering more children?

Obama's father was an inveterate alcoholic who was involved in numerous automobile accidents. His driving record shows that in one accident he lost a leg; in another accident he killed someone. In 1982 after getting drunk he drove into a tree and killed himself. Perhaps his dream was to be reincarnated as a dolphin swimming in a sea of martinis?

Obama Sr. was also a socialist and anti-neo-colonialist who supported the so called African National Liberation Movement of the 1970s. This ideologically communist movement was aimed at liberating African countries from the economic domination and political influence of Europe. After African countries achieved their independence from the Europeans in the mid-1960s, colonialism, as we know it, was a thing of the past and a new form of struggle for independence emerged. The colonial powers maintained economic and, to various degrees, political interests in their former colonies in terms of the means of production, primarily concerning mining.

The European countries and corporations had the capital and, more importantly, the expertise to manage enterprises efficiently, while the former colonies provided the manpower to operate the facilities. The former colonies were getting the benefits in the form of royalties, taxes and local employment. Therefore, any conflicts between the parties were expected to be primarily economic; but instead, the conflicts became political and military affairs.

It is important to point out that the African National Liberation Movement was a political as well as a military movement. The political philosophy behind the movement was that the former colonial powers got rich through their savage exploitation of colonies and the development and sale of the former colonies' natural resources. Therefore, they should redeem the forgiveness from former colonies by paying them back for the stolen goods. The movement had nothing to do with liberty and everything to do with power and other people's wealth.

It was no coincidence that this movement was supported by massive military deliveries from the Soviet Union and the intervention of Cuban combat forces equipped and trained by the Soviets. The Soviet Union used the movement to establish a strategic platform for ideological and military expansion into Africa.

In Angola, the Soviets concentrated 300 hundred tanks and 60 helicopter gunships supported by 15,000 Cuban troops prepared to invade neighboring countries in a massive way. The situation began to accelerate to the point of potential disaster for moderate African states.

Kenya's legendary President Jomo Kenyatta, himself a leader of the anti-colonial movement in Kenya who wrested Kenyan independence from the British Empire and who had enormous influence in Africa, opposed the Soviet intervention and requested help from the United States whose geopolitical interests in containing the proliferation of communism coincided with the preservation of an independent Africa.

The United State initiated covert operations to provide military assistance to African regimes. Although American assistance was on and off, and, as usual, often became a victim of partisan bickering in Congress, it did halt Cuban expansion in Africa. The war went on for 15 more years until Ronald Reagan decisively kicked the Cubans and their Russian masters completely out of Africa.

Now, in this context, we can get a clearer picture of Obama Senior's actual dreams; America was preventing the spread of communism in Africa, America is evil! Capitalism is a tool of exploitation! The future is with socialism! That would explain why Barack Obama joined Jeremiah Wright's church and was listening to Jeremiah Wright's disgraceful displays of anti-Americanism and his hatred of white people for 20 years. *Jeremiah Wright was singing the song of his father.*

When Barack Obama says he does not remember his spiritual mentor's outrageous comments about this country, I am sure he is telling the truth. When you are continuously listening to something that is part of your own thinking, a part of your psyche, you pay little or no attention it being repeated by somebody else. I am sure that when Mr. Wright was exclaiming "Goddamn America" or talking about the CIA spreading the AIDS virus among blacks—that was nothing new and controversial to Mr. Obama. Therefore, he heard and he didn't; he was and wasn't there. And that's exactly what he is saying: he wasn't there. In Islam they call it Taqiyya[2].

We should take the President at his word. That is the only plausible explanation for the controversy.

Perhaps Obama Senior's dream was to liberate Africa and the rest of the world from imperialism, colonialism and capitalism in order to create a Marxist paradise of working and exploited people of the world? And what if that dream cannot be realized as long as America, a bastion of capitalism, is there.

Which one of those dreams would President Obama like to implement?

Socially, the President is the total opposite of his father. He is a devoted family man, faithful husband and loving father. Although the President smokes, he is not a drinker.

We will leave it to the readers to complete our deductive approach and decide for themselves what dreams of his father the American president dreams of implementing. But let us take this even further.

This begs the question:

What about Obama's dreams from his mother? She had a lot greater influence on little Obama than his far away father. Barack Obama referred to his mother as "the dominant figure in my formative years ... The values she taught me continue to be my touchstone when it comes to how I go about the world of politics."

His parents were ideological twins. They got to know each other while attending a Russian language class. The

Russian class really caught my attention. Why were those two learning Russian in the 1960s? My Eastern European suspicion tells me that they were planning to enter the University of Patrice Lumumba in Moscow.

This so-called People's Friendship University was an educational and research center founded in 1960. Its stated objective at the time was to help nations of the Third World, mainly in Asia, Africa and South America by providing higher education and professional training. In reality the University was preparing leaders of the National Liberation movement. The students were indoctrinated in Marxism/ Leninism.

There is a good reason to believe that Obama's mother would continue to instill the ideology of his father into her son way after they divorced. When her son's convictions were challenged by his step-father, Sutoro, she sent her son from Indonesia, where they lived at the time, back to Hawaii to live with his grandparents. She was definitely concerned about preserving the seeds of Marxism she so successfully planted into his brain from the heresies of her new husband.

In Hawaii, Obama was accepted in the 5th grade at Punahou School, once known as Oahu College, one of the best private schools in the country. The education does not come cheap—just for comparison, the 2011–2012 tuition is $18,450. In this case, like so many others throughout

Obama's life, we do not know who paid for the expenses. But that is another story.

I would only partially agree with that assessment of Messrs. Gingrich and Dinesh D'Souza (who wrote a book about Obama, "Roots of Obama's Rage", that was made into the hit movie, "2016") that "the most accurate, predictive model for his behavior" is Obama's anti-colonial views.

Colonialism was a thing of the past by the time our President was born. His values could have been shaped instead by anti-neo-colonialism, the movement that took place after Africa secured its independence. As we noted earlier, anti-neo-colonialism was a Marxist movement inspired and supported by the Soviet Union. The final objective of the movement, there should be no mistake, was the establishment of Marxist governments in Africa.

We may dispute whether for Obama "the most accurate, predictive model for his behavior" is anti-colonialism, Marxism, or both, but what is not in dispute is that the model for his behavior is not Americanism.

Is Obama a Socialist?

Bill O'Reilly says that Obama is not a socialist because he does not advocate the expropriation of private property. Mr. O'Reilly describes Obama as an ideologue. So do a lot of other people who have never been exposed to or are only vaguely familiar with the economic theory and philosophy of socialism. But if Mr. Obama is an ideologue, as Mr. O'Reilly believes he is, than what ideology does he adhere to?

Whether a person is a socialist or not cannot be judged by this single criterion alone. The problem is that there is no one universal model of socialism. As a political philosophy socialism offers up a huge variety of entrees for every political taste. It includes, but is not limited to, state socialism, democratic socialism, social democratic social-ism, National Socialism, Christian Democratic Socialism, Soviet style revolutionary socialism and so on.

The difference between these political flavors is in the type of social ownership they advocate, the degree to which they rely on markets versus planning, management of economic enterprises, and the extent of government involvement in ownership and regulation of enterprises. But they all have one thing in common; fair and equitable distribution of wealth within the society.

In his book "To the Rural Poor" Lenin stated, "*We want to achieve a new and better order of society: in this new and better society there must be neither rich nor poor; all will have to work. Not a handful of rich people, but all the working people must enjoy the fruits of their common labor. Machines and other improve-ments must serve to ease the work of all and not to enable a few to grow rich at the expense of millions and tens of millions of people. This new and better society is called socialist society. The teachings about this society are called socialism.*"

"This is the moment when we must build on the wealth that open markets have created, and share its benefits more equitably," Barack Obama said.

Although, it may sound rhetorically somewhat different from Lenin, philosophically they are identical. Both quotes mean taking as much money as possible from productive citizens to share with the non-productive.

In order to implement the egalitarian dream, socialist society does not necessarily require the ownership of the means of production. As we pointed out earlier, there are different versions of socialism and most of them would address egalitarianism maintaining private ownership of the means of production. Governments have a variety of means to enforce the distribution of wealth accumulated by private enterprises. Among the most powerful tools, besides such extreme methods as expropriation and nationalization, there are taxation and regulation. Private enterprises can simply be regulated and/or taxed into equality.

I call this version of socialism, Obamanism. It calls for high taxes and excessive regulation. Regardless of strategy, the final outcome is to enable the so-called working people to enjoy the spoils of egalitarian society. Western Europe is a prime example.

The Soviet version of socialism, revolutionary socialism, on the other hand, was based on Marxism and the expropriation of private property by the State as well as the complete abolition of private enterprise by force. Nevertheless, even hardcore committed socialists can tolerate a little private enterprise for a while.

The Russian Bolsheviks are a case in point. In order to restore the economy after the war and following the revolution, the Bolsheviks enacted NEP (New Economic Policy) which was introduced in Russia in the 1920s in order to get Russia out of its economic depression. This new policy lifted restrictions on private property and allowed private enterprises into the economy. As soon as the country started to recover, the Bolsheviks imposed heavy taxation on private enterprises and drove them out of business.

North Korea is another example; I am sure most of us think of North Korea as a Communist State that forbids private property and outlaws the free market. You may be surprised to know that approximately 75% of North Koreans are independent contractors. After a famine in the mid-1990s where a million people died, the government decided to lease the means of production to private entre-preneurs. Officially, everything belongs to the government; but in reality private businesses run the industry and pay bribes to government officials.

Obama's background and affiliations leave no doubts about this President's political pedigree. Since his early years Barack Obama has sought out and maintained relationships with radicals, communists, socialists and anti-capitalist groups that shared his views.

Today, President Obama has surrounded himself with self-professed communists, socialists, Mao Zedong admirers, anti-free marketers, Constitutional revisionists and supporters of big government and the welfare state. They exhibit scant respect for the Constitution and the rule of law and share the familiar attributes of Marxist-socialists.

Given his agenda, like Universal Healthcare, huge proliferation of the welfare state, Cap and Trade Bill, tons of additional regulation and heavy taxation supplemented by attacks on the private enterprise system, the President would fit in comfortably in France, with the Socialist Party, socialist government, socialist president and socialist country.

So, if we ask the Europeans, as I did, about Obama, they point out the undeniable fact that President Obama is positively, definitely another democratic socialist.

However, if you are willing, once again, to look at the President through my Marxist red glasses you will see that his ideology has a lot more in common with Karl Marx and Vladimir Lenin then with Pierre-Joseph Proudhon[3]) or Francois Hollande[4]).

Chapter Four

The Politics of Morality

"The great corporations of this country were not founded by ordinary people"

"You Didn't Build That"

I have to confess when I heard that Obama said that, I thought it was taken out of context. Only after I read it myself did the significance of what the President said settle in. It was totally unexpected from the President, who is a disciplined politician. I bet you that from now on he sticks to the teleprompter.

This statement is so revealing that I decided to quote the entire statement so I would not be accused of taking anything out of context. The following is a perfect example of Bolshevik demagoguery and lies. Mr. President, Lenin and Trotsky would be proud of you. This is a case of the loyal student besting his teachers. They could not say it better.

> *"If you've been successful, you didn't get there on your own. You didn't get there on your own. I'm always struck by people who think, well, it must be because I was just so smart. There are a lot of smart people out there. It must be because I worked harder than everybody else. Let me tell you something—there are a whole bunch of hardworking people out there.*
>
> *If you were successful, somebody along the line gave you some help. There was a great teacher somewhere in your life. Somebody helped to create this unbelievable American system that we have that allowed you to thrive.*

Somebody invested in roads and bridges. If you've got a business, you didn't build that. Somebody else made that happen. The Internet didn't get invented on its own. Government research created the Internet so that all the companies could make money off the Internet.

The point is, is that when we succeed, we succeed because of our individual initiative, but also because we do things together. There are some things, just like fighting fires, we don't do on our own. I mean, imagine if everybody had their own fire service. That would be a hard way to organize fighting fires.

So we say to ourselves, ever since the founding of this country, you know what, there are some things we do better together.

That's how we funded the GI Bill. That's how we created the middle class.

That's how we built the Golden Gate Bridge or the Hoover Dam. That's how we invented the Internet. That's how we sent a man to the moon.

We rise or fall together as one nation and as one people, and that's the reason I'm running for president— because I still believe in that idea. You're not on your own, we're in this together."

The President has accidentally unlocked a window into his soul. What he is saying is; "You did not build it alone, you should not own it alone," or, more to the point: "We build it collectively, we own it collectively."

There are two types of society, each based on very different premises. One is: "You built your business; therefore you own your business"; and the other type of society, says" If you built your business, you built it because of our collective effort and, therefore, we all have to share it."

The first type epitomizes "can do" individualism and is inspired by American Idealism. The other one embodies the Marxist/ Leninist philosophy of parasites.

This latter philosophy is all too familiar to former Soviet citizens, "If you made a scientific discovery, invented a new technology, or wrote a book—it is not your accomplishment. The government educated you, provided office space and laboratories. It does not belong to you, it belongs to the society. This psychological axiom of fairness has been a way of life for primitive tribal societies for thousands of years and was adopted by the Bolsheviks, and now, as we discovered, by our President who has primed it for this country.

I was amused that the President contrives that "you succeeded because you got help" and points out that "there are a whole bunch of smart and hardworking people" who did not succeed. If we drive the President's statement to its logical conclusion we shall conclude that if you are not successful it is not your fault; you just did not get help. Therefore, society must compensate you for your misfortune.

This reveals a startling reversal of the ideology of the Democratic Party, as so eloquently expressed by another democrat and great American, Daniel Patrick Moynihan, who said,

"The great corporations of this country were not founded by ordinary people. They were founded by people with extraordinary intelligence, ambition, and aggressiveness."

The President himself has had many great teachers in his life, no doubt; judging by his philosophy and actions, the two most gifted being Marx and Lenin. As I stated earlier, it should come as no surprise that he believes that the true origin of wealth is the exploitation of working people. In order to restore the equilibrium of fairness, the owners (the Rich) have to transfer their unfair share of wealth back to society. The Russian Bolsheviks called it, "Expropriation of expropriators." In effect, the President who keeps talking about going forward is building a time machine to take America back to the socialist future.

The President is desperately trying to substantiate his argument for the fairness of wealth redistribution. But he is not doing a very good job. His statement is full of factual inaccuracies and insinuations. First, the implication that the government built capitalism is simply false. As I will discuss at greater length in a later chapter, government had nothing to do with the industrial revolution that precipitated the development of capitalism. The subsequent transformation of society has been taking place without government leadership, mandates or any substantive State involvement.

Or take this one:

> Somebody invested in roads and bridges. If you've got a business, you didn't build that. Somebody else made that happen. The Internet didn't get invented on its own. Government research created the Internet so that all the companies could make money off the Internet.

This is ridiculous, if not sardonic. The last time I checked the Constitution it was "we the people" who established the government and enumerated its powers granted under the Constitution. Hence, the government is just a hired manager to perform certain "enumerated" functions. It is founded and supported with our tax dollars. We "the people" invested in the country's infrastructure, roads and bridges and we made that happen. Government only administered the contracts—not even managed it. It was private enterprises that managed, engineered, supplied equipment and materials and actually built it. It is a monument to American ingenuity and the power of private enterprise.

We all use it and we all are still paying for it in form of gasoline tax and tolls where applicable. The President mentioned that the government invented the Internet. That is a distortion of the facts. He is not the first to claim this honor. Al Gore did it before, but that does not make the President's statement any less ridiculous. Government played an important role, as it has with the development of many other things that revolutionized human life, but it is individuals who deserve the credit.

Here's another fallacious statement, "That's how we funded the GI Bill. That's how we created the middle class." Did the GI Bill create the US middle class? That implies that there was no middle class in the US prior to the mid-1950s.

The historical truth is that the middle class emerged in the 18th century as a by-product of the evolution of capitalism that lifted millions of people out of poverty. Not through government welfare, not by government handouts or due to the redistribution of somebody's wealth, but through the rise of productivity of capitalist enterprises and the hard work of millions of people engaged in trade, commerce and other productive activities. It does not matter to the President that the statements he makes are untrue. He knows if he repeats them often enough, with the passion and intensity of Leon Trotsky, it may became true. It worked for the Bolsheviks.

No civilization in history be it Romans, Greeks, Persians or the Soviets has been able to provide the sort of upward mobility for every segment of society that the Western economic free market model has done. All of the foregoing civilizations had their own governments. But the men who created the American system of government understood the undeniable truth that innovation and prosperity come from individuals, not from the government. Individualism is the essence of American Idealism.

However, our President is promoting collectivism when he says, "I still believe in that idea. You're not on your own, we're in this together."

The ideology of collectivism has existed in varying degrees around the world, and is present in political movements like socialism, communism, and fascism. It is deeply embedded in Judaism and Islam. For the masses it creates an unfounded expectation to succeed collectively when they failed individually. Collectivism trumps the individual's rights in favor of the interests of society; and, shifts moral and social responsibilities from the individual to the State.

The Soviet Union enacted a "liberal interpretation of law in favor of society." In plain English, regardless of the individual's rights under the law, in the final analysis if there is a conflict of interests between an individual's right and the interests of the State, the court ruling shall be in favor of the State.

Collectivism is replacing individual responsibility with collective responsibility. It works both ways; nobody personally is responsible for anything or we are collectively responsible for the fault of an individual. The President uses the concept of collective responsibility all the time. It is Bush's fault, it is the Congress' fault, and it is the financial crisis that did it or European crises.

The Bolsheviks extended the concept of collectivism to new dimensions. In the extended version, collectivism was not limited to the collective ownership of property and every individual's way of life; it also included an institution of collective responsibility. Indeed, when Bolsheviks applied their fairness doctrine, they applied it to classes: proletarians (working people) and the bourgeoisie (capitalist class). The concept justified communist repression against groups of people and against whole classes of the population.

The President's propensity for authoritarianism can explain why our Neo-Bolshevik is dividing the country between the 1% and the 99%. He is trying to convince the nation that demonizing and suppressing one percent of the citizenry (just three million people) is no big deal and is fully justified; while doing so in favor of 99% of the people. To get the support of the 99% at the expense of the 1% is also a canny political choice. But it is a slippery slope.

Hence, he hopes that the 99% of togetherness will resonate with the American people. Together, it sounds great. No one wants to be alone. Obama is artfully playing on human insecurity, indulging their hopes and fears.

I expect this kind of rhetoric to intensify and gain more support in the coming months, particularly from the Left and members of the 'Occupy movement."

Obama's Fairness Doctrine

In his State of the Union address the President laid out his vision of America. "We can either settle for a country where a shrinking number of people do really well, while a growing number of Americans barely get by," he said. "Or we can restore an economy where everyone gets a fair shot, everyone does their fair share, and everyone plays by the same rules."

I have to admit those words rankle me, setting off my Eastern European suspicion. Every time I hear "fairness" from a politician, I grab my wallet and get ready to move my assets overseas.

Why? Because I am tired. I am tired of hearing that old socialist song about the inequities of capitalism. I am tired of listening to our President talking about fairness and everybody playing by the same rules. I heard this song for thirty years in the Soviet Union.

I am tired of hearing the President demonize people who pay their taxes lawfully and then get criticized for not paying enough. I am tired of politicians helping the middle class and saving Social Security. I am tired of promises now to be fulfilled later. I am tired of mediocre lawyers and unemployable Bachelors of Arts insulting my intelligence.

As an university professor once said to his students, "If you cannot express yourself in numbers, you do not know what you are talking about."

It is no surprise that the President has failed thus far to define fairness in numbers. It cannot be defined; fairness is one of the most subjective of philosophical notions. Fairness in politics has always been, and remains, pure demagoguery, a way to provide a moral justification for those of limited abilities to "demand" according to their unlimited needs.

You cannot create fairness, even God could not do it: he created an unfair world. Life is unfair: some people die young, children get cancer, some are born beautiful or rich, or both, and some neither. Fairness is not a right, or a privilege. Fairness is not something one can legislate.

Fairness is a moral concept. A doctrine that promotes fairness is an excuse to override the rights of individual and to override law. Any government interference that attempts to substitute the law of the land with a fairness doctrine will eventually lead to the destruction of society. The role of government is not to impose its interpretation and enforcement of fairness; the role of the government is to enforce the law.

The President says that everyone should play by the same rules. It is a novel idea especially coming from this government.

Oh, yes, as the Russian poet put it, if you want to be right, do not turn to the left; if you want to have a queen next to you, try to be a king yourself first.

So let's start close to home. If everyone should play by the same rules, then elected officials should start living by the same rules that apply to the rest of us.

Consider OSHA, Occupational Safety and Health Administration, whose regulations do not apply to the government.

The Freedom of Information Act which specifically excludes government departments.

And what about financial regulation? It is very telling that the Sarbanes-Oxley Act does not apply to Congress. The Act requires the chief executives of public companies to certify their financial reports and, in a case of providing false or inaccurate information to the public they could be fined up to $5 million and serve as many as twenty years in prison. Members of Congress (like all federal officials) are making up numbers as they go, passing laws based on false data, misleading the public without any sanction what so ever.

Or perhaps the President's "fairness" speech was talking about General Motors' bailout? As a result of this so-called managed bankruptcy, the bondholders were shafted in favor of the United Auto Workers union and the union pension fund received preferential treatment in violation of the Bankruptcy Law.

On a final note, how does Affirmative Action fit with an economy where everyone gets a fair shot and everyone plays by the same rules? What does it tell you about this country and our black President's vision?

"Affirmative action" means positive steps taken to increase the representation of women and minorities in areas of employment, education, and business from which they have been "historically excluded." Those steps involve *preferential* selection — selection on the basis of race, gender, or ethnicity.

As a result, white applicants with good grades are not accepted in universities because universities receive bribes in the form of federal and state benefits, for admitting minorities regardless of their grades. This is not so different from the way qualified Jewish students faced discrimination in the former Soviet Union.

Furthermore, Affirmative Action requires the government and large corporations to put aside a number of contracts for minority businesses. Here, again, we see a pattern of awarding contracts to incompetent black and other minority contractors on a strictly racial basis. Did I say incompetent? Of course, if they were competent, they would not need preferential treatment.

The whole idea of preferential treatment should be insulting and demeaning to blacks and other so-called minorities. It sends a subliminal message that these people are inferior and need government assistance. It is morally wrong and it is wrong on substance. When was the last time Jewish people, who have been discriminated for centuries, including in this country, asked for preferential treatment? What they have always demanded is equal opportunity to compete. Given an opportunity, they were confident that they could blow the competition out of the water.

This confidence has helped the Jewish people survive under the most gruesome circumstances.

I remember my second day in the United States, we had a briefing at HIAS, a Jewish organization that helps immigrants to settle in the United States. "Perhaps you think that there is no anti-Semitism in this country," we were told, "but you are wrong." The beauty of this country is that you may be turned down for the job because you are a Jew, but you can apply across the street and be accepted because you are a Jew." It was fair enough for us. Thousands of Jews who emigrated from the Soviet Union, most of whom did not even speak English, succeeded beyond anyone's dreams.

If the President is sincere when he says he wants to have an "economy where everyone gets a fair shot" he should take advice from the Chief Justice of the United States, John Roberts, who said, "The way to stop discrimination on the basis of race is to stop discrimination on the basis of race."

The President's public speeches about fairness and the alleged deficiencies of the American capitalist system have never translated into sound economic policy. Even his most powerful arguments about fairness don't hold water. He says it is fair for the rich to pay more. Why it is fair? The rich did not get rich by paying less; as a matter of fact they have always paid more. According to the IRS the top 1% contributes 37% of all taxes collected and the top 10% pays 50% of all taxes. At the same time the lower 50% pays nothing. How is this fair? It is their country too.

As we said earlier, the President fanatically believes in his own righteousness and superior intellect. Perhaps, we the ordinary folks should entrust our lives to him so he can determine the rules and dole out our fair share. Perhaps, our President will become the "Father of the People," like comrade Stalin, who called Soviet people the screws of the state mechanism. And was Stalin ever right: We all turned in the same direction, we were inserted where our Father wanted to insert us and we were removed when he decided that it was convenient for him. And in the end, we were totally and completely screwed.

The American constitution grants all citizens the same rights under the law. It prohibits discrimination based on race, gender and religion. That is what gives all of us a fair shot at the American dream, including for our first black President.

The American people don't need a "fairness doctrine" to grant what they already have. The President and the country would be better served if the President committed himself to protect the basic rights spelled out in the Declaration of Independence and the Constitution, instead of "fairly" violating the rights of some people in order to benefit others.

For the sake of fairness he should make government live by the law of the land and make use of his personal example to empower black people to aspire to their full potential.

What is Fairness, Anyway?

The current Presidential rhetoric about fairness and calling for the rich to pay their fair share, reminds me of a story about the Jewish gangster Misha Yaponchik who operated in the Russian city of Odessa in the early 1920s.

Misha was an ordinary robber who invented racketeering in Odessa. Instead of robbing his victims Misha decided to tax businesses. He did not offer protection; he just promised not to rob them in the middle of the night and not to use violence if payments were remitted to him in a timely manner. Misha kept half of the proceeds for himself and members of his gang; and the other half, he distributed among the poor in the form of food and other necessities. In this way, Misha administered fairness by asking the rich to pay their fair share.

Misha Yaponchik was not a well-educated young man; he was not familiar with the basics of "progressive" economics. It never occurred to him that by taking money from the rich and giving it to the poor, he was stimulating the economy. The NKVD, the People's Commissariat of Internal Affairs (secret police), did not share those economic theories either; they had Misha shot. If not for this unfortunate event, Misha Yaponchik, today could qualify for a Nobel Prize in economics.

Odessa's businessmen celebrated Misha's death prematurely. Shortly thereafter, the NKVD arrested the exploiters of the working people, expropriated their "means of production" and sent them to Siberian labor camps, where most of them perished. That was the Bolsheviks' fairness.

It makes me wonder, if the President wins re-election and gets a chance to implement his fairness doctrine of wealth redistribution, is he going to be Misha Yaponchik or the NKVD?

Chapter Five

The President's Energy Policy: "Oil, Money and Solar Power"

The Stone Age didn't end because we ran out of stones

The Church of Global Warming

"This is the moment when we must come together to save this planet. Let us resolve that we will not leave our children a world where the oceans rise and famine spreads and terrible storms devastate our lands," the President proclaimed. "The Apocalypse Now" is threatening a host of calamities unless we spend more money.

The Vice-President was not far behind, just as persuasive but less vivid, "I think it is manmade. I think it's clearly manmade. If you don't understand what the cause is, it's virtually impossible to come up with a solution. We know what the cause is. The cause is manmade. That's the cause. That's why the polar icecap is melting." Joe Biden said, outlining the administration's position on Global Warming. Although the Vice-President sounds terminally confused, if he says, "I think it is manmade," then there should be no more debate. It is settled. We should take it as gospel and blow trillions of dollars in an effort to save the planet. And according to the President, this is it. There will not be another moment. Do it now!!!

I am old enough to remember that, not so long ago, in the mid-1970s the world debated 'global cooling' with the same intensity as we are debating global warming today. It was also very urgent and potentially catastrophic although, back then, we needed to save the planet from freezing.

In 1975, the Newsweek article "The Cooling World" suggested cooling "may portend a drastic decline for food production." A 1974 Time Magazine article "Another Ice Age" painted a bleak picture for the future of our planet. I recently raised this argument with a supporter of global warming. His response was that science is a lot better today than it was forty years ago. "Does it mean that the science was wrong in predicting a new Ice Age?" I asked him. He did not respond, but I got my answer. It really does not matter what the science says: we just must believe in global warming.

Since Galileo's time, ideology has always tried to overtake science; and it often has. It may be because it's more convenient for human nature to acquire wisdom from prophets, rather than bother itself with facts and scientific analysis. Therefore, the three elephants that used to support planet Earth are frequently coming back.

Thinking about this, I finally realized that the struggle over Global Warming is becoming a religion. It teaches us that Mother Earth may soon crack under the weight of our environmental sins, but "three elephants": Al Gore, Leonardo Dicaprio and John Travolta, will keep the Earth from sinking into the abyss if we follow them and don't ask questions. And so, the Church of Global Warming was formed.

Like every religion, it has spawned extremists demanding an Inquisition. Today, this Inquisition is headed by former Representative Patrick Kennedy, who once announced that anybody who does not believe in Global Warming is a traitor and should be treated as such.

As we all know, religious fanatics usually demand full

and complete obedience from their followers. The followers, in turn, must demonstrate that they are "more Catholic than the Pope." As a result, stupid things are proclaimed true, billions of taxpayers' dollars are spent on absurd projects, and close supporters of the administration get rich—very rich.

The importance of the theology of Global Warming for the President's strategy of re-engineering America cannot be underestimated. It provides a foundation for at least two out of the three pillars of his strategy: 'Destruction of Wealth' and the replacement of a 'Capitalist Market-Oriented Economy' with a 'Government-Controlled Political Economy'.

Global Warming justifies unlimited expenditure, strangles oil and gas production, practically stops coal mining, and puts power generation under tight government control.

It also puts a lot of money into the hands of Obama supporters. People like Al Gore, who are managing exchanges of the so-called "greenhouse gas emissions," stand to make an enormous amount of money, literally out of air, by underwriting the sale of "carbon credits" that industries, utilities, and other entities must purchase for the "right" to operate their facilities, which produce industrial emissions.

In addition it would create alternative energy industries that cannot exist without government subsidies. The fundamental aspects of the President's strategy are organized around Global Warming. In 2008, the Obama-Biden comprehensive 'New Energy for America' plan (at a cost of $150 billion over the next 10 years), promised, among other great things, to create five million new green jobs as well as put one million plug-in electric cars, that can get an equivalent of up to 150 miles per gallon, on the road by 2015.

It was Then and it is Now

CBS News counted 12 clean energy companies that collected billions of dollars in federal assistance, and are now in trouble. Five have filed for bankruptcy: The junk bond-rated Beacon, Evergreen Solar, SpectraWatt, AES' subsidiary Eastern Energy and Solyndra.

Widely advertised as one of the administration success stories, Amonix, a solar panel manufacturing plant in North Las Vegas, was heavily financed under an Obama administration energy initiative. Recently, it closed its 214,000-square-foot facility, only 14 months after it opened. Solar Trust filed for bankruptcy protection recently. The company has held rights for the 1,000-megawatt Blythe Solar Power Project in the Southern California desert, which last April won $2.1 billion of loan guarantees from the administration. The list goes on....

According to a new report by Pike Research, a Boulder, Colorado-based clean-energy market research firm, given current trends in sales, the goal of one million plug-in electric cars will be not attained before 2018.

The whole Global Warming affair and the romantic dream of alternative energies reminds me of the famous scene from Molière's "Le Bourgeois Gentilhomme," in which M. Jordan, the play's hero, is trying to improve his intelligence by taking writing lessons. He requests his teacher help him with a love note. The teacher asks whether he wants the note to be written in poetry or prose. M. Jordan replies that he doesn't want either. The teacher explains that it has to be one of the two because they are the only ways to write. M. Jordan admits to his teacher that he is quite surprised by the fact that he has used prose for forty years without knowing it.

The supporters of Global Warming and stated advocates of alternative energy recite the poetry of dreams without any awareness that there exists a prose of reality. The President and his supporters believe that we use a lot of hydrocarbons, which emit CO_2 and cause Global Warming. According to them, we must make a transition to clean, alternative, or renewable sources of energy. However, we may be quite surprised to find out that they do not even know what hydrocarbons are.

Appearing on NBC's "Meet the Press," former speaker of the House Nancy Pelosi suggested that natural gas—an energy source she favors—is not a fossil fuel.

"I believe in natural gas as a clean, cheap alternative to fossil fuels," she said at one point. In the words of Samuel Johnson, "Such an access of stupidity … is not in Nature."

Going from metaphor to renewable energy, it cannot go unnoticed that the President and his supporters talk a great deal about renewable energy, but don't know that, for the foreseeable future, there is no practical way for renewables to replace oil, coal, gas, and other hydrocarbons which provide 90% of our energy supply. Or do not care to know—which may lead us into a real manmade, actually the President's made, calamity.

In the face of insufficient energy supply and hostile environmental regulation, the economy faces the danger that it may go into a tail spin of protracted depression. Yet, as we demonstrated earlier, the president is ideologically a Marxist and, like all Marxists, he is dogmatist. Dogmatism is a form of philosophical idealism, which makes conclusions first and then selects facts to support its earlier conclusions. Moreover, it is not just an omission of relevant data; it is also a refusal to accept objective reality as well.

When during a recent speech in Virginia, Obama announced that he will "double down" on his green energy efforts, we should not be surprised. It only epitomizes his dogmatism. Since the President has accepted the postulate of Global Warming and accepted that the phenomenon is manmade and the source of the problem is hydrocarbon, he cannot be persuaded to change course regardless of the prose of reality.

Not to be confused as M. Jordan was, I decided that it may be about time to sort out the poetry and prose of Global Warming and alternative energy.

To Be or Not to Be

Since most of us lack the intelligence of Mr. Biden, let's first separate poetry from prose.

First, is there Global Warming?

Second, if it is, is it manmade as Mr. Biden suggested?

Third, can we do anything about it?

Fourth, is alternative energy a solution?

Contrary to this administration's pronouncements, the science about this issue is not settled. Although, many scientists, the environmental movement, and most of the media are committed to the theology of Global Warming, the science does not validate its existence. The administration's argument that the majority of the science community or how they call it "the scientific consensus" supports Global Warming is totally irrelevant. Scientific disputes are not settled by majority consent; otherwise we would have outlawed the laws of gravity.

The majority has been proven wrong more times than not throughout history. Just remember a few heretics like Galileo Galilei, Nicolaus Copernicus, Albert Einstein, or the most recent example, Global Cooling, which was also supported by the majority of scientists.

There is no convincing evidence that Global Warming exists as a permanent phenomenon, rather than being just a 40-50 year cycle as some scientists believe. At a time when Nancy Pelosi is declaring Greenland a global warming disaster, it is worth remembering that the island was covered with forests when the Vikings (or Norse) settled the region and created a farming community six hundred years ago. She may also be surprised to learn that the

Romans grew grapes in northern England. Hence, the temperature on this planet was a lot higher then.

Did I mention that back then neither Romans nor Vikings had oil refineries and coal fired power plants? Since no modern scientific model can explain the change (from then to now), the science is just not reliable when it comes to the change of temperature on this planet. We have to conclude that: we do not really know whether there is Global Warming.

In case nobody noticed, the disciples of Global Warming are not sure the planet is warming either. Since the appearance of some evidence lately that suggests the planet may be cooling, they have stop calling it "warming." They now prefer calling the phenomenon "Climate Change"—just in case. Although they are not sure what it is, the ambiguity does not deter them from insisting that it is still manmade or that we have to spend money to save the planet.

The Theater of Absurdity

The absurdity of Global Warming does not stop here. Let's assume, for the sake of argument, that there is a long trend and that this planet is getting warmer. There is no compelling evidence to suggest that the source of this phenomenon is CO_2 gas (carbon dioxide). There are other persuasive causes for global warming. The sun's activity and the earth's reflectivity could affect temperature on this planet.

The only reason CO_2 was identified as the source is because the dogmatists had decided that Global Warming must be manmade. Since most of CO_2 gas is produced by motor vehicles and the industrial production, the choice was obvious.

Hence, if the United States will replace internal combustion engines with electric power trains and restrict emissions from our industrial and coal fired power plants we will save the planet. There is a reason I keep emphasizing the United States; other countries, especially the major polluters like Russia, China, and Eastern Europe have no intention of following this destructive path. Every single week of the year, China brings into service a new large coal-fired plant that has, practically, no air pollution controls and that, coming from Asia, subsequently contributes to 30% of the air pollution in Los Angeles.

By taking this position, the supporters of Global Warming demonstrated that they have no idea as to how scientific data is collected, analyzed, and utilized. If they did, they might've found that their theory of Global Warming is full of holes and has not been proven. Recent fires in Southern California demonstrated that Mother Nature can produce in several days an amount of greenhouse gases larger than that generated by all the cars in the region in a whole year. California's yearly fires have been known, since the Spanish Conquistadors first visited in 1542. If we add volcanoes spitting into the air millions of tons of carbon dioxide every year for thousands of years, then according to the proponents' theory, we should all have already being living on small islands surrounded by an ocean of melted arctic ice.

The conclusion: There is no evidence that CO_2 gas (carbon dioxide) is a source of Global Warming. Although, it is a major source of the air pollution, there is no solid evidence that it is having an impact on the Earth's temperature one way or the other. Therefore, it is not manmade and there is nothing we can do about it.

So, what about the alternative energies? The administration holds a dual position on the subject. They are trying to convince the American people that alternative energies will alleviate the danger of Global Warming while simultaneously wanting to reduce our dependence on foreign oil. The problem with their pursuit of alternative energy is that solar power generation, where the administration has invested most of the taxpayer's money, simply does not work on a large commercial scale. It lacks "commercially proven" technology and, in its current form, is unreliable and incompatible with conventional sources of energy such as coal, oil, gas, nuclear, or even wood chips.

To make the situation even worse the President appears to be pursuing two mutually exclusive objectives. As we stated earlier the President plans to put a million electric cars on the road; and that will require an increase in power generation to support this additional consumption.

At the same time, in a June 9, 2011 press release, American Electric Power's Chairman and CEO, Michael G. Morris, stated: Because of compliance with the new EPA regulations, we will have to prematurely shut down hundreds of good power plants, nearly 25 percent of our current coal-fueled generating capacity.

The future markets took notice. Electric grid operator PJM recently held a capacity auction and the price for 2015 will be $136 per megawatt, eight times higher than what was paid for 2012, according to *Investors Business Daily*. In the regions where coal-fired plants are being retired, such as in northern Ohio, the rates are as high as $357 per mega-watt. Thus, instead of increasing the generation of electric power to support additional consumption, the administration is planning to dramatically reduce existing capacity.

Without having a realistic program to replace the retired generating capacities and address additional demand, the administration is creating an artificial energy crisis in this country.

Now we understand what is happening. The administration is investing enormous resources to solve a problem that does not exist with a solution that does not work and in the process is manufacturing an energy crisis in this country.

Furthermore, Global Warming is one gigantic fraud, which among other things, is designed to scare the public and redistribute wealth from the taxpayers to the rich cronies of the President and his party in order to make them very rich.

How It all Began

Here is the real truth about the Environmental movement that I learned while at the University of Marxism/Leninism.

In the early 1960s, General Charles de Gaulle, then president of France, was concerned about the United States' industrial domination, which at the time consisted of almost 50% of the world's output. One of his ministers came up with the idea that the more a country produces, the more it contributes to the world's pollution. The idea that industrialization had a detrimental impact on the planet was not new, having been around since the Industrial Revolution. However, the possibility of turning this concept into a set of international agreements that would alter American economic expansion and diminish its political influence on Europe was appealing to de Gaulle who was always envious of the United States. This was a low risk endeavor for France. France's economy was in shambles after the war, so any environmental limitation on their industry would have a negligible effect.

The Soviets embraced the concept with a great deal of enthusiasm. They shared de Gaulle's concern but for different reasons. The United States was a preeminent economic and military power. The Soviet Union saw the United States as a formidable opponent in their quest for the proliferation of communism in Western Europe and other parts of the world. The U.S. was a military-industrial giant who had proved to be a decisive factor in winning the Second World War. They possessed nuclear weapons and would not hesitate to use them. Accordingly, the Soviet Union was eager to support anything that would undermine the United States economically and politically. The potential impact of such treaties on the Soviet economy was not a concern, as the Soviet Union never abided by any agreement, as a matter of policy, if it was not in their national interest.

The Soviets loved the idea so much that they financed the environmental movement via Western European communist parties up to the late 1970s. After the demise of the Soviet Union, funding dried up, but by then there was a whole new generation of fanatics to do the Soviets' job. The 1970s industrial pollution scheme evolved into an even bigger scheme: the Global Warming movement. Ironically, the Soviets are no longer around to enjoy the spoils of their investment.

That is how the West has been had

Albert Einstein used to say, "The definition of insanity is doing the same thing over and over and expecting different results." The American people would like to know how many times President Obama must take the taxpayers' money and loan it out to clean energy companies and expect different results. Or, perhaps, he doesn't. The Neo-Bolsheviks will succeed regardless whether or not the alternative energy program is successful.

As we stated earlier, the first pillar of Obama's strategy requires him to spend money and the alternative energies are just as good a way to waste money as condoms or manure management. Whether the continuation of govern-

ment investment in alternative energies is a manifestation
of the President's dogmatism or just a shrewd strategy to
spend more money, or both, we will never know.

The Magic of Oil

*"We can't have an energy strategy for the last century
that traps us in the past. We need an energy strategy
for the future—an all-of-the-above strategy for the 21st
century that develops every source of American-made
energy."*—President Barack Obama, March 15, 2012.

"They would not have believed that the world was
round," Obama said. "We've heard these folks in the past.
They probably would have agreed with one of the pioneers
of radio who said, 'Television won't last. It's a flash in the
pan. One of Henry Ford's advisors was quoted as saying,
'The horse is here to stay but the automobile is only a fad."

Unless anyone is in doubt I am compelled to inform
you that President Obama is not Galileo, or Henry Ford, or
one of the inventors of television. If anybody wants to trap
this country in the past it is this President, whose socialist
agenda and Bolshevik philosophy of a government-controlled economy, epitomizes the ugly socialist past.

Unfortunately, the President's energy strategy does
not go beyond ridiculing his opponents. He succeeded in
converting the fundamental concept of physics [energy]
into political demagoguery. His speeches do not generate
any substantive debate because there is no substance in the

President's oratory. Instead of offering a logical and factual explanation of his position, the President offers empty rhetoric and a distortion of his critics' position.

I am an engineer by training. Unlike politicians, engineers use logic and numbers to defend their position. First, why is it that we cannot continue an energy policy that brought unparalleled prosperity to this nation and built the most powerful economy in the world? Second, if you can convince me with science and numbers that we do have to change, what are our options and what is the cost?

As I said earlier, if one cannot express himself in numbers he does not know what he is talking about. Since the President has no numbers and no facts to support his position I am going to offer facts, numbers and logic to demonstrate the unsustainability of the arguments offered by the supporters of alternative energy.

Fossil Fuels

My questions to the President and his supporters are: What is wrong with fossil fuel? What is the most compelling argument to spend trillions of dollars to replace the sources of energy that served us so well for the last hundred years?

The President's principal arguments are: the necessity of new sources of energy because the reserves of fossil fuels are diminishing and Global Warming is reaching a disastrous level.

Both arguments are demonstrably wrong.

Let's take the diminishing supply first. It is worth pointing out that concerns about oil are not new. As early as 1885, various experts cautioned that oil would soon be depleted. The State geologist of Pennsylvania warned that "the amazing exhibition of oil was only a temporary and vanishing phenomenon—one which young men will live to see to its natural end." The experts were proved wrong back then, just like they were proved wrong in the 1970s and they are being proven wrong today.

Today this country and neighboring Canada are blessed with plentiful energy resources: oil, gas and coal. Advances in the techniques of horizontal drilling and hydraulic fracturing, first applied to shale gas reserves, are now making it possible to develop US oil in reserves that, previously, were commercially unviable. In the last few years, the United States surpassed Russia as the largest gas producer in the world.

America is sitting on top of a super massive 200 billion barrel Oil Field that could potentially make America energy independent and that, until now, has largely gone unnoticed. Thanks to new technology, the Bakken Formation in North Dakota could boost America's Oil reserves tenfold, giving Western economies a trump card against OPEC's short-term squeeze on oil supply; and making Iranian and Venezuelan threats of disrupting oil supplies, irrelevant. We should also add Texas, Louisiana, and the Gulf Coast, extending inland through west Texas, Oklahoma, and eastern Kansas have important reserves. There are also significant oil fields in Alaska along the central North Slope.

There is nearly 200 billion barrels in oil reserves—almost equal to that of Saudi Arabia—to market from land-locked Alberta.

As far as Global Warming is concerned the previous chapter exposed the fraudulent nature of the theology.

Fossil fuel, however, is not clean energy. It has serious side effects; it pollutes the environment. The real issue is whether it is even possible, not mention practical, to replace fossil fuel for strictly environmental reasons, given the state of technology and the constantly growing demand?

What are commercially viable alternatives? The diagram below from the U.S. Energy Information Administration tells the story in numbers.

U.S. Energy Consumption by Energy Source, 2009

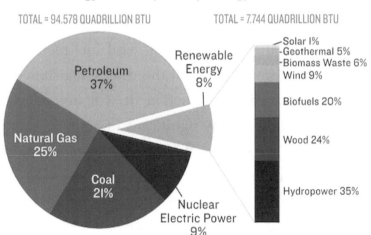

TOTAL = 94.578 QUADRILLION BTU   TOTAL = 7.744 QUADRILLION BTU

Petroleum 37%

Natural Gas 25%

Coal 21%

Nuclear Electric Power 9%

Renewable Energy 8%

Solar 1%
Geothermal 5%
Biomass Waste 6%
Wind 9%
Biofuels 20%
Wood 24%
Hydropower 35%

Source: U.S. Energy Information Administration, Annual Energy Review 2009

What this diagram tells us is that more than 90% of our energy consumption (biomass included) is provided by fossil fuels. The major energy component of all fossil fuels is carbon. Therefore, one does not have to be a nuclear scientist or brain surgeon to conclude that our civilization is solidly carbon oriented, and, unless we decide to return to caves, that picture cannot be altered significantly in 10 or 20 years' time. Given the current energy demand to power this huge sixteen trillion dollar economy and constantly growing appetite for more energy, realistically speaking, there is no way the situation can change significantly over the next 50 years.

Does that mean that we shouldn't or couldn't move from carbon to other types of energy? No, it doesn't. But when we do move, that change is not going to come from the government—just like fossil fuels were not invented by government. Therefore, illiterate environmental fanatics can write all the poems they want about Global Warming but it will not affect the prose of fossil fuel reality that is here to stay. Regardless of all the drastic legislative measures to curb carbon production, it will not reduce the world's carbon use by any significant amount.

Can we at least reduce the fossil fuel component in our energy consumption?

Let's examine our alternatives and try to find out what might work, what might not, and let's do it using a logical deductive approach.

Hydropower

Hydropower is a very clean method of producing renewable energy, and Mother Nature takes reasonably good care of supplying enough rain to run hydroelectric plants. However, the potential for building more hydropower plants in the US is basically exhausted. Hydropower plants need two components: a natural water stream, such as a river; and a water reservoir, such as a lake. The lake is formed by a dam and that requires huge amount of land in order to hold a sufficient amount of water to equalize its use. Good examples are the Hoover dam in Nevada and dams on the Columbia River in Washington State.

However, there is a rare consensus between engineers and politicians that here, in the US, we have already exhausted the land necessary for a substantial plant, or the land that would have to be flooded (and its residents relocated). Accordingly, the current level of hydropower use cannot be substantially increased.

Geothermal power

Geothermal power uses hot water and steam coming from the depth of the earth where radioactive decay of various particles creates hot spots. Except natural geysers of the sort we can see in Yellowstone Park, in order to tap geothermal power, we need to drill deep wells and pump hot streams to the surface. There, the steam and hot water are used in the steam turbines to produce electric power.

Despite the expense of drilling and cleaning underground water and streams, and despite the high corrosiveness of those streams, it is still economically advantageous to use geothermal energy whenever we can find it within reasonable depths. However, the potential for geothermal installations is relatively small and most of the streams get depleted with time. So, even if we double our current use of geothermal energy, it still will be a negligent amount in our energy balance.

Solar Energy

Solar energy generated a lot of promise. Solar plants are being built at an accelerating pace in Europe and the United States. Improving technologies have been developed that make solar production more economical than they were in the 1980s when the first large-scale solar plant was built in the Mojave Desert in California. However, the fundamentals of solar energy production that limit its use have never changed—it is difficult to transmit the energy produced. No solution has yet been invented and unless we find a way to transmit energy wirelessly by a microwave link like cellphones do, the potential for solar energy remains limited.

The fundamental problem with solar energy is that it must have sunlight as a fuel. Even in the southern hemisphere, usable sunlight exists for no more than 10-11 hours per day. Since we cannot store large amounts of electricity, solar plants are only operable for about half of the day.

That said, they still could be able to contribute to satisfying our daily peak usage that typically occurs around noon, especially in the summer when air conditioning use increases.

Nevertheless, we cannot consider solar installations as a reliable power source, because they are subject to interruption of power production at any time. I personally observed the complete shutdown of solar production at the plant in Mojave Desert, when a small cloud drifted across the sun. Consequently, solar power requires standby capacity that can support the grid 24 hours a day. Utilities do not advertise that, but when they contract to buy power from solar sources they quietly build in adequate fossil fuel backups capable of bolstering the solar supported load. The other inherent problem with solar power is its high maintenance requirements.

All solar installations rely on a system of mirrors that concentrate the sunlight on a target that becomes heated and transfers that heat to a working fluid such as water. The mirrors have a tendency to get dirty and in the desert, the most advantageous place to build is in the sand. The average solar plant has thousands of mirrors and the task of cleaning those mirrors takes time, reduces power production, and involves significant costs. Besides, sand storms, frequent in the desert, can damage the mirrors to a degree that makes their effectiveness very low.

Capital and maintenance costs would make construction of the solar plants prohibitive if not for the huge subsidies that States have legislated under pressure from environmentalists. I am not aware of a single solar plant that did not go bankrupt when the subsidies ended.

Biomass

Biomass is a viable prospect. Biomass is the waste from agricultural products. It is burned in boilers, and the produced energy is converted into electric power. We have a number of biomass plants in this country. In the past agricultural waste and even forest chips were burned in open fields generating huge amounts of pollution. Burning waste in modern boilers, where pollution can be efficiently cleaned, provides clear benefits to society.

However, biomass is still a carbon based fuel and it produces CO_2 as every fossil fuel does. Besides, it is highly unlikely that we will double agricultural production in the foreseeable future. Therefore, we shouldn't expect the share of biomass in our energy balance to change.

Ethanol

Ethanol is an alcohol-based fuel made by fermenting and distilling starch crops, such as corn.

Creating plant-based biofuels requires too much farmland to be practical or sustainable—land that would be better used to grow food.

Producing ethanol and other biofuels takes more energy than the fuel can generate.

"Ethanol is too expensive to be used as a fuel," an industry source said, adding ethanol cost four to five times more than petroleum as a raw material.

Regrettably, there is no good idea that government can't turn into failure.

Wind Power

Wind energy's major drawback is the same as solar; the so called dispatch-ability, i.e. the ability to get such power at any time and in predictable and reliable quantities. So far, because wind power production varies due to the availability of wind, utilities cannot count on it as a reliable source of energy. Because we cannot store any significant amount of electric energy today (and probably won't be able to in the foreseeable future), wind power production must have a backup especially during peak hours.

Consequently, when utilities buy wind power from suppliers, they must quietly provide a fossil fuel backup, using mostly fast-starting gas turbines burning (guess what?) natural gas. There are some exotic technologies that wind power producers have been experimenting with, such as building Compressed Air Energy Storage (CAES) plants along with wind power facilities.

The technology for CAES has existed since early 1980s. The idea is simple: during the hours when all energy produced by wind cannot be consumed, the excess of power is used to compress the air and pump it to underground caverns such as salt domes and abandoned mines, which would serve as energy storage. During peak hours, when there is a big demand for power, the air is released and heated using a small amount of natural gas. Heated air drives a turbine and produces electric power. Another simple idea that proved to be too complicated and impractical.

Nuclear Energy

Nuclear energy is among those energy sources producing very low levels of carbon dioxide emissions from their full life cycle. It is closely comparable with renewables such as wind, solar and hydro in this respect. However, the same people who advocate for a clean environment aggressively opposed this reliable, cheap and safe type of energy resource. I said safe because it enjoys an almost impeccable safety record.

Nuclear reactors are routinely used for aircraft carriers and nuclear submarines that travel all over the world. Nuclear power is a major generator of electricity in Western Europe. It is responsible for producing 78% of the electricity in France, 43% in Belgium, 36% in Spain and so on. The opponents of nuclear power believe—and I say believe because the data tells us otherwise—that nuclear power poses a threat to people and the environment.

They point to three nuclear accidents that have taken place over the last forty years: The Three Mile Island accident in 1979 that resulted in no damage or injuries; the self-inflicted Chernobyl disaster in 1986; and Fukushima

Daiichi nuclear disaster in 2011, which was exacerbated by the reactor being improperly located and poorly designed.

China has 25 nuclear power reactors under construction, with plans to build many more. Although, nuclear power is proliferating, marching its way around the globe, local "true believers" of environmental policy will not be persuaded by the facts. Nuclear energy is truly an environmentally responsible source of energy but the environmentalists violently oppose it. Therefore, nuclear power is out.

Given the prose of reality, what is the President going to do? He will do what he does best: Talk.

The prose of reality is that fossil fuel or hydrocarbons will maintain their economic and strategic significance way into the 21st century. The most significant being oil. Oil is the biggest business and the largest industry in the world in terms of assets, capital and overall importance. With the exception of computers, the oil industry has been the source of most important innovations in the areas of technology and manufacturing. No other industry is big enough and strong enough to address the economic and population growth of the 21st century.

Chapter Six

Capitalism

The purpose of the capitalist economy is to create wealth

Preview

Growing up in the Soviet Union gave me a unique perspective on capitalism and contemporary American society: on the one hand, the official stance of the Party and its followers was relentlessly negative; on the other hand, if you knew how to read between the lines, as my father often taught me to do, you could divine the great strength and vast opportunities of the American capitalist system. So, for example, when Pravda, the official Communist newspaper, trumpeted that U.S. Steel production was only a small fraction of what the Soviet Union produced—and then you applied that information to the U.S. population (which was significantly smaller than that of the Soviet Empire), you understood that American was booming in construction and other steel-dependent enterprises.

Among engineers, there is a saying that a country's level of science and technology is in direct proportion to the number of floors in its buildings and the level of prosperity is proportional to the number of cars on its roads. By both these criteria, the "decaying" capitalist America was light years ahead of the "advanced" Soviet economic model.

Ironically, the current attacks on capitalism in its nature and veracity are identical to the communists' propaganda employing similar metaphors like exploitation, inequality, system abuse, pyramid schemes, and environmental Armageddon etc. To the Soviets, Capitalism was the 'root of all evil'.

By contrast, the critics of capitalism never speak of such "great accomplishments" of socialism as the environmental disasters in the Soviet Union that exceeded anything we know in terms of human suffering and untimely deaths. You never hear American liberals talking about the socialist labor camps where an estimated twenty million people gave their lives building the 'Great Projects' of Communism. You never hear about reversed river currents that caused drought, famine, and starvation. No one speaks of human rights abuses in Socialist countries.

Since economic activities do have side effects it is easy to select those examples that best serve the propaganda purposes and sell it to the public as an inherent flaw of the system. Since capitalism or the free market economy is a vital part of American society, any attacks on our economic system should be treated as an attack on the society as a whole. In the next chapter we will talk about capitalism, its accomplishments such as providing the opportunity for universal prosperity, advancement and the basic elements and services that we take for granted every day of our lives. From soup and cotton to passenger jets and iPods, from polio vaccines to heart transplants, capitalism has done it all. From companies started in family garages to giant corporations' industrial plants and laboratories around the world, no other system has produced such innovation and such positive results for individuals as well as for humanity.

No other society conceived itself as a product of exceptional entrepreneurship in pursuit of excellence— rewarded when it succeeds and punished when it fails.

Karl Marx had it Right. Really?

Capitalism is moral and represents the ultimate expression of our rights of "Life, Liberty and the pursuit of Happiness" as written in the United States Declaration of Independence. Those rights are the essence of individual freedom.

Although Karl Marx has been completely discredited even in the eyes of even hard-core liberals, there are some people—including members of the current U.S. administration—who are using this current economic crisis to actively promulgate his socialist ideas. Despite the serious perils of socialism, which some do admit, they argue nonetheless that capitalism has not worked well lately either; and that government involvement is necessary to alleviate what they perceive as deficiencies in the free enterprise system. The recent financial crisis and following recession reignited the debate about the sustainability of the free market capitalist system.

The financial crisis created a panic among economists and politicians of both parties and opened the flood gate to new, or, in most instances, forgotten—ideas. There is no shortage of publications, opinions and proclamations that the American Dream is slipping way, that the middle class is under pressure; that it is more difficult than ever to reach middle class status (whatever that may be since there is no universal definition of middle class).

"While we believe that capitalism is fundamentally superior to any other system for organizing economic activity, it is also clear that some of the ways in which it is now practiced do not incorporate sufficient regard for its impact on people, society and the planet," Al Gore said.

The former CEO of Goldman Sachs Asset Management, David Blood, said capitalism has been blighted with short-termism and an obsession with instant investment results, which had ramped up market volatility, widened the gap between rich and poor and deflected attention from the deepening climate crisis.

Even such a respected American economist as Nouriel Roubini, who anticipated the collapse of the U.S. housing market and the worldwide recession that started in 2008, told the Wall Street Journal:

"Karl Marx had it right. At some point, capitalism can destroy itself. You cannot keep on shifting income from labor to capital without having an excess capacity and a lack of aggregate demand. That's what has happened. We thought that markets worked. They're not working. The individual can be rational. The firm, to survive and thrive, can push labor costs more and more down, but labor costs are someone else's income and consumption. That's why it's a self-destructive process."

In the Journal, Roubini argued that the U.S. economy is flagging because businesses are hoarding cash—more than two trillion dollars by one estimate—rather than investing it in factories, new equipment and hiring workers. As he put it: "If you're not hiring workers, there's not enough labor income, enough consumer confidence, enough consumption, not enough final demand. In the last two or three years, we've actually had a worsening, because we've had a massive redistribution of income from labor to capital, from wages to profits." "Markets aren't working," Roubini concluded.

Roubini is not alone in his assertions. Paul Krugman, a Nobel Laureate in economics and supporter of Keynesian Economics, believes that government involvement in the current economic crisis has been insufficient and he has been calling for another ever greater stimulus package and broad government involvement in the economy.

Robert Reich, political economist, secretary of labor under President Clinton believes that government spending, high taxes and big government are actually good for the economy and he is not alone.

Those who are ignorant of history or who have a short memory, are proposing a new economic idea—the planned capitalist economy. Some are going even further offering a political (socialist) economy. Some favor a mix of some capitalist principles with government regulations to prevent crises and recessions and to ensure more adequate distribution of wealth. Haven't we heard this before?

To enhance the credibility of their arguments some economists on the left have been touting their Nobel laureate status, but that speaks more about the Nobel Laureate

Committee than the quality of their ideas. If Karl Marx
were alive today he would be a Nobel laureate for economics many times over. Today, 150 years after his death,
Marx is not only remembered, he is widely studied. Who
will remember the current crop of geniuses twenty or thirty
years from now?

During the years since Marx's "Kapital" was published
in 1867, there has been no shortage of critics of capitalism
and several generations of supporters of socialism, many of
whom have grown up to fight literally and figuratively for
the utopian promised land of a social paradise and economic justice. So, Messrs. Roubini, Krugman, Reich, Blood
and Gore are in good company.

The opponents of capitalism are using the current
crisis to rail against alleged flaws of the free market. They
are blowing out of proportion certain flaws as symptoms of
serious deficiencies that can only be addressed by government control and regulation. They are looking for villains
in incompetent CEO's, greedy bankers, unscrupulous fund
managers, market speculators and crooks like Bernard L.
Madoff. This is the excuse for the legislature to get busy
making new laws and tough regulations intended to
prevent abuses and protect average investors in the future.

The idea that the capitalist system can be improved by
the government, or any other single entity, is pure fantasy.
The unique feature of capitalism is a collective genius of
millions of entrepreneurs, managers, traders, scientists,
engineers, technicians and workers making billions of deci-

sions every second around the globe with one purpose and one purpose only: to make money.

To believe that anyone has the capacity to understand the intricacies of the movements of capital, and can positively affect those movements and is also able to distribute the proceeds of trades and profits fairly (whatever that means), without distorting the markets and creating economic and social chaos, is a veritable absurdity.

Capitalism is an intricate economic system that does not result from a single event but rather has evolved over the centuries. Thus far it has demonstrated an extraordinary fortitude and resilience in overcoming a host of crises, economic downturns, the Great Depression, world wars, natural disasters, and many other calamities, while improving and transforming itself into a more vibrant and more productive system resulting in the most progressive upward surge of wealth in history.

Capitalism established its overwhelming superiority after World War II. The defeated countries of Germany and Japan which were completely obliterated and whose economies were destroyed adopted the free market economic model. Twenty years later, those countries were rebuilt and prosperous. By contrast, the Soviet Union which was victorious in the war proceeded with a socialist economy as did its Eastern European satellites including East Germany. However, twenty years later they were still in the ruins of economic stagnation. These two examples provide a stunning demonstration of economic realities.

Was Karl Marx right? Are markets not working? Why

do economic crises occur and can they be avoided? What is the role of government in avoiding economic downturns or in stimulating the economy to alleviate a crisis once it develops? And finally what is the path forward?

The Centuries of Emancipation

I decided to Google capitalism. After reviewing a dozen or so definitions of capitalism, I chose one by Rosemary Peavler, a professor from Morehead State University: "Capitalism is an economic system that emphasizes private ownership of the means of production or a privately controlled economy. In a capitalist society, you have a free market and companies live by the profit motive. They exist to make money and maximize the wealth of their owners or shareholders, whether they have one shareholder or thousands. Prices, production, and the distribution of goods are determined by competition in a free market. There is supposed to be a limited regulatory framework. It is envisioned that legislation defines and enforces the basic rules of the free market. The government does provide some public goods and services as well as support."

Well, I could not have said it better myself. I would like to emphasize "a limited regulatory framework." Unfortunately, this fundamental postulate seems to be long forgotten.

So, what is wrong, if anything, with this system; and why do some people believe that capitalism has not worked well lately?

First, what do we mean by "lately"? Are we talking about the last two years, twenty years, or two hundred years? We have to realize that capitalism is an economic system in permanent evolution. Over the centuries it has evolved from the era of slavery which continued for thousands of years, and the breakup of feudalism into a private enterprise system that created more overall wealth during the last 200 years than was created over the preceding 7000 years of human civilization. That would suggest that capitalism has, overall, worked pretty well.

Any major shift in productivity and subsequent creation of wealth has been associated with capitalism. Capitalism was the driving force behind the Industrial Revolution, telephone communications, computers, commercial Internet, nuclear energy, and many more breakthroughs. If not for capitalism, we would still be riding in carriages, sailing oceans in wooden ships, and using an abacus.

For thousands of years, handicrafts were the only method of production known to man. One thing made at-a-time, was a slow and labor-intensive process. With the development of the industrial revolution and the invention of steam and electric-powered machines, productivity was raised exponentially and mass production of goods and services became possible.

Mass production allowed the easy expansion of manufacturing, creating an economy of scale that provided supply at a lower cost to meet demand. The economy began producing more and more goods and services and doing so at constantly diminishing costs.

As efficiency was rising, competing enterprises could sell their products at lower prices. Unlimited supply of goods and services at lower price contributed to a higher standard of living. In an effort to further reduce costs, more and more sophisticated machinery and methods of manufacturing were employed, resulting in a continuing rise in productivity.

At the same time, mass production required skilled labor, engineering and technical support. As the cost of production was going down the cost of labor was going up. Higher wages translated into greater consumer purchasing power. The society of mass productivity and mass production was born, which had an enormous impact on the economy, society, and our way of life. Mass production stimulated the development of a society of mass consumption, which resulted in a new class of citizenry—the modern bourgeoisies or middle class—that is the economic backbone of this country.

> "America's abundance was created not by public sacrifices to the common good, but by the productive genius of free men who pursued their own personal interests and the making of their own private fortunes. They did not starve the people to pay for America's industrialization. They gave the people better jobs, higher wages, and cheaper goods with every new machine they invented, with every scientific discovery or

technological advance—and thus the whole country was moving forward and profiting, not suffering, every step of the way."

Thus wrote a Russian immigrant, novelist-philosopher Ayn Rand, almost 50 years ago in her splendid book, "Capitalism: The Unknown Ideal."

At every step along the development of capitalism since its birth in Europe, we have seen the evolution of the relationship between labor and capital. The labor-intensive enterprises of the industrial revolution required huge labor resources that the cities of European countries could not supply until thousands of illiterate peasants migrated to the cities. Seeking opportunity, they were willing to accept any working condition in exchange for what they saw as a secure income. This created a new class of labor that Karl Marx called the lumpen-proletarians, saying they had "nothing to lose but their chains."

The last two hundred years of economic expansion have been characterized by an enormous rise in productivity and wealth. This period of mass production and mass productivity was marked by a concentration of wealth among the upper economic echelon of the society— i.e., capitalists, the owners of the means of production. This period was also characterized by the ruthless exploitation of workers: twelve-hour work days, no health insurance, no safety regulations, and no vacations.

The concentration of wealth at the top, and miserable living conditions at the bottom, inevitably led to a conflict.

Mass production requires mass consumption to maintain balance, but when commerce began producing more goods than could be consumed, economic crisis inevitably followed.

When Henry Ford was making more cars than he could sell, he raised the pay for his employees. With the introduction of assembly lines and Taylor's management techniques, Ford managed to lower the cost for his Model "T" to the astonishing price of $290 per car, a price that his workers and thousands like them could afford. Production went through the roof and so did the profits of Ford Motor Company.

Every crisis was followed by further expansion, innovation and a rise in productivity. Higher productivity resulted in higher income and lower production costs making goods and services increasingly more affordable.

I call it "the cycle of prosperity": The affordable automobile changed America; it put the country on wheels. The automobile erased boundaries between cities and suburbs, improved deliveries of goods and services, and created a host of new industries. It was just the beginning.

Over time, the masses (lumpen) of proletarians became organized into labor unions. The unions' contribution to the improvement of working conditions, to further increasing productivity, and to helping create more financial security among the working people cannot be overstated. The continued increase of wealth elevated the lumpen-proletarians into bourgeoisies who had properties and means of production—and had a lot to lose. Contrary to

Karl Marx's prediction that the proletarians would have to rise in violent struggle to be liberated from poverty, the emancipation of working people has been accomplished through the evolution of the capitalist system as an economic necessity.

It is important to point out that all these transformations of society took place without government mandates, involvement, or even encouragement.

This period also marked humanity's most rapid and sustainable advances in living standards and life-opportunities.

The Spiral of Evolution

The role of government in the development of capitalism resembles the story about the three kinds of people:

There are three kinds of people: those who make things happen—capitalists; those who watch things happen—the most of us; and, those who look at things happening and wonder, "what the hell is happening?"—that would be government.

Government, which had nothing to do with the rise of capitalism, noticed after a while that something was happening, that a great deal of wealth was being created and the government was not getting its unfair share. What did they do? "Let's regulate and tax it and distribute fairly." At that point, so many years ago, Henry David Thoreau's maxim that, "the government is best which governs least" was sent to collect dust on the shelves of history.

Unlike a planned socialist economy, or what some economists called a "command and control economy," which is based on underproduction and inventory control to ensure constant demand for goods and services, regardless of quality and price, the free market capitalist economy is unregulated and based on overproduction. Overproduction creates competition and operates on the assumption that products and services of the best quality and lowest cost will outperform those of lesser quality or higher cost.

Regardless of what triggers a recession, the underlying fundamental is overproduction, which is the result of excess inventories and excess of capacity. Until the excess inventories are worked out and excess capacity is eliminated, the recession will continue.

If inventory cannot be sold in a reasonable period of time, production has to slow down and the labor force must be cut to reduce the output. Reduction in the labor force results in diminishing purchasing power for consumers. This cycle feeds itself: diminished consumer purchasing power leads to further cuts in economic output, which leads to further reductions in the labor force, which leads to still further diminished purchasing power and thus to an additional reduction in consumption...and so on until available capacity and production are balanced with demand. This vicious circle will continue until inventory excess is sufficiently reduced to create a new demand. Then a new cycle kicks in: produce, employ, prosper, and overproduce until the next crisis.

As long as the "survival of the fittest" is in place, weak

enterprises perish, while the strong, more productive and better capitalized grow stronger. Old and outdated industries die and new businesses and industries, offering new goods and services, are born. Though painful to endure, economic crises serve as a self-cleansing mechanism to rid the marketplace of fat and inefficiencies, making enterprises that survived the downturn leaner and more productive. Some call the process "creative destruction." A new economic structure will rise from the destruction with new industries offering products and services that most of us could not even envision.

The private enterprise system, like anything alive, can fall ill from time to time; yet in the process of recovery can transform itself into a more vibrant and more productive system by eliminating waste and improving its business model. During the recovery, the system develops immunity against a particular bacterium, grows stronger and gains more strength and resilience with each new "bug" it fights off.

As long as the capitalist system is alive, it will progress from crisis to crisis, constantly improving itself and ultimately increasing wealth and prosperity for all.

It is essential to understand that the current crisis is not a deviation from the established order or from the quintessential principles of capitalism but rather a temporary disturbance in the economic equilibrium and a product of the evolution emanating from successes and failures.

The great evolution of capitalism did not stop in 2008. On the horizon a new form of capitalism is already emerging. One of the elements of this new form is the "Built-to-order" concept that has spread like wildfire.

Far superior to anything before, it does not require inventory, warehouses, offices or even stores. The products and services are sold in virtual stores over the Internet as the march of capitalism continues around the planet, evolving into new forms, new business models offering new products and services at a lower cost. And so it goes.

As stated earlier, the most essential source of upward mobility for millions of workers is an inherent conflict between labor and capital. A constant source of conflict is the struggle for a greater share of profits generated by the rise in productivity. The relationship has evolved from employment-at-will to partnerships, from proletarians without means of production to the self-employed and employees having a stake in enterprises. In any case, the conflict is always there.

During a downturn the conflict is exacerbated by hardship and should be addressed so that the spiral of evolution continues. Today's economic crisis is no exception.

Labor unions are a prime example of the constant transformation of our economic system. They are also at the root of the current economic crisis. In this instance, labor unions, as we stated earlier, have contributed enormously to shaping the capitalist economic system—ending exploitation of children, protecting workers from industrial hazards, improving productivity, and raising wages—but have also, over the course of time, priced themselves out of the market. At that point they became an impediment to progress and to further improvements in productivity.

When labor unions exhausted their usefulness, they became a drag on the economy, bankrupting cities, states, and industries. Teachers' unions prevented meaningful educational reform, thus contaminating the American labor pool with illiterates. Manufacturers' unions demanded wages and benefits that made American products uncompetitive with non-union foreign enterprises. American companies, in order to survive, are now compelled to move their operations outside the States, which causes further declines in U.S. manufacturing jobs.

We Want to Help

Excessive government regulation may contribute to downturns as well. There should be no doubt about the benefits and necessity of government regulations, especially covering product safety, protection of the environment, child labor etc. However, we must be mindful that all regulations do have side effects. The problem is that government bureaucracies have no boundaries and no sense of proportion. Furthermore, bureaucracies are incapable of evaluating the ramifications of government regulations on efficiency and competitiveness.

Usually, the unintended consequences only became evident after a regulation is fully implemented. Many regulations are intended to regulate past abuses already addressed by capitalism through crises. Unethical businesses and the individuals who commit them are not likely to repeat scams that have already been exposed. Those regulations created to address past abuses are ineffective and only increase production costs, making products less competitive. US Government keeps piling on regulations that increase the cost of doing business and in many instances greatly restrict businesses ability to continue operations.

Several utilities including American Electric Power, Duke Energy, and Southern Company recently announced they are closing coal-fired power plants. This was due to new EPA regulations that would add excessive costs to meet the new standards. The results: layoffs, higher electricity prices and the possibility of power outages.

Businesses that manufacture motor fuel will pay about $6.8 million in penalties to the Treasury because they failed to mix a cellulosic biofuel into their gasoline and diesel as required by law.

The problem is that cellulosic biofuel is not commercially available.

There are also high efficiency toilets that do not work, light bulbs that are expensive and contain heavy metals that make them hazardous and difficult to dispose. The list of the US Government regulations that impede business and complicate the lives of American citizens could be a few miles long.

The counter-productiveness of government regulations is not limited to the United States. On the other side of Atlantic, where socialist governments have been in power for decades, government regulations have reached the point of ultimate absurdity. In Spain agricultural regions have been turned into deserts because farmers are paid for producing no crops. In Italy fields that used to grow crops are covered with solar panels that do not generate power because there are no buyers—yet the land owners still collect lease payments. In Germany, the power utilities are obligated to buy electricity from individuals who generate power from solar panels at a premium over the cost of electricity. The Russian immigrants there, who have great deal of experience with socialism, supplement their incomes by using electric lights to light the solar panels at night. They sell the produced energy back to the power companies and collect the difference.

Myths & Fallacies

A widely held fallacy is that during recessions small businesses are inevitably hailed as the key to recovery and showered with still more targeted programs. The role of small business in the overall economy and employment is widely misunderstood.

While statistically small businesses create most of the jobs during a recovery, it is big business that moves a big economy. Only when big business starts increasing capacity, making investments in new buildings, equipment and facilities, and subcontracting jobs to small enterprises does the wealth subsequently begin trickling down to service industries and lead to significant increases in employment.

It is said that "a rising tide lifts all boats." Businesses like mine do not make tides but when companies such as Exxon and Chevron start making waves, we will be taken for a ride. And, we will get our piece of the action. We will increase our staff and more people will join the ride and the pizza parlor on the corner and the dry cleaner in the shopping center will get their share and so on.

Another myth supported by some Nobel Prize economists on the left and subscribed to by the current administration is that government can create productive jobs that are associated with making profits. These supporters insist that the government should be operated as a business.

The dichotomy here is that business is all about making money while governments are all about spending money. The government, by its nature, is a "not for profit" enterprise and supposed to invest in goods and services that, although not productive, are necessary for the public good and that private enterprise would not invest in, like defense, public transportation etc.

During a recession, politicians talk a lot about legislating incentives for job creation. It is another case of emphasizing the obvious over the important.

The purpose of capitalism is not job creation. The purpose of the capitalist economy is to create wealth. Employment and the subsequent distribution of spoils of an economy is a byproduct of capitalism.

Economic growth creates the need for more workers.

The government's job is not to ensure full employment or the reduction of unemployment; the government's job is to provide legislative and regulatory conditions conducive to economic expansion. The rest will be taken care of by the free market.

The conventional thinking of some modern economists and of this administration is that the economy could be reignited by the government investing in infrastructure—building roads, dams, airports etc. and education. The evidence does not support this theory. The Obama administration has already spent $800 billion of public money on a stimulus package that included "shovel ready projects" and education. Was anything built with this money? The "shovel ready" projects turned to be not so "shovel ready" and American education shows no improvement after spending billions of dollars. Not a scintilla of improvement.

Undaunted, the President has called for another round of stimulus spending directed at the public sector and hiring more police officers, fire fighters, teachers etc. The first stimulus bill directed huge resources toward the preservation and generation of public employee jobs. At least a quarter of all the money was directed to states or cities to preserve government jobs and to create new public sector jobs. In this respect, it did bring down the unemployment numbers. It is hard to disagree with the President that without the stimulus the unemployment numbers would be even worse and the economy would look even grimmer. But the bottom line is, although that the stimulus perhaps made the President look not as bad he would without it, it has done nothing to stimulate the economy.

Somebody forgot to tell the President and his advisors that a capitalist economy is not built with government money. The only way to get a capitalist economy going is to incentivize private investment. Putting more people on the government's payroll will not move the economy forward; actually, it will have exactly the opposite effect. As the stimulus runs out, it will require more government spending or higher taxes to support new hires resulting in less profit for the businesses. It will actually de-incentivize private investment.

If our past experience is any guide, the government's ability to create productive jobs outside of labor camps is extremely limited.

Accordingly, the argument can be made that, in most cases, the government is an impediment to job creation. If history has taught us anything, it's that government intervention in the economy has consistently produced negative results. There is an abundance of evidence of how the government's interference produced catastrophic or near-catastrophic consequences. During the Great Depression, government interference only increased the pain, deepened the impact and prolonged the suffering. During the 1970s Arab oil embargo, Jimmy Carter's interference into the oil market, imposing price controls, only exacerbated the situation.

Similarly, government intervention into the current recession, including the bailouts, economic stimulates, mortgage discounts and quantitative easing, arguably distorted the marketplace and prolonged the crisis, positioning the country on the verge of bankruptcy. The policy of the current administration, of bailing out of the called "too big to fail" firms, helps preserve unprofitable firms, in a manner that only hides the system's inefficiency and delays the inevitable.

Making Capitalism Work

Now, the questions that must be considered are: What is the role of government? Is there anything government can do to prevent a recession? Is there anything the government can do to get us out a recession? Shall government promote, subsidize or finance business ventures or projects they believe may stimulate the economy or do public good?

I know what my readers are thinking, because the question "what is the role of government" has been debated since the writing of the Declaration of Independence. Well, I do not pretend to know all the answers but do believe the following responses to be valid.

Is there anything government can do to prevent a recession? The answer is: No.

Since 1807 we have had at least ten significant recessions, some very serious like the Great Depression. With each downturn government involvement in the economy has grown and the numbers of laws and regulations has been expanding exponentially. But the recessions continue, on average, every twenty years.

Following World War II, the federal government passed legislation that essentially said "it's the policy of the federal government to try to prevent recessions." Based on the statistics above, figuratively speaking, the government was trying to prevent the law of gravity. Market forces are too complex and are a lot stronger than any government's ability to control them. As a matter of fact, it is beyond anybody's ability to do so including God's.

Agony of Impotence

The administration's latest attempt, outlined on September 8, 2012 in Obama's speech before the Congress, was more an exercise in ideological passion than a coherent strategy. It failed to define the national purpose and contained no effective long-range economic policy. The President, who says we cannot look to the policies of the past, failed to articulate his policies and vision for the future.

The government has a foggy understanding of economic fundamentals otherwise they would realize the hopelessness and absurdity of their intervention in the marketplace. The government's approach has thus far boiled down to saving incompetent, criminal, or just obsolete business models and "too big to fail" corporations with an infusion of the taxpayer's money collected from productive citizens and successful enterprises to keep losers afloat.

Politicians don't like unemployment, and it certainly hurts their reelection prospects but they can't prevent it either.

The objective reality is that regardless of bailouts, restructuring, loans etc. governments cannot stop the permanent evolution of capitalism. It cannot prevent the inevitable and only extends the agony of impotence. Enterprises that cannot compete or have exhausted their useful life will die and be replaced by new businesses who have adapted to a new business environment.

The current administration's efforts to influence market forces have been an exercise in futility.

During the last four years, the administration has taken a number of actions aimed at restoring economic equilibrium. None of them have worked as intended and have arguably worsened the situation. The stimulus package, cash for clunkers, the release of oil strategic reserves in an attempt to manipulate the price of oil, quantitative easing, mortgage refinancing, tax credits for new home buyers, bailouts—these efforts have failed miserably. Furthermore nobody can account for $800 billion of stimulus money that disappeared in a black hole of government ineptitude and corruption.

The administration's struggle have reached the point of veritable absurdity as the President and his allies try to convince the American public that unemployment benefits and welfare checks are forms of economic stimulus. Millions of people are currently receiving welfare checks, food stamps and extended unemployment benefits. The only positive effect unemployment benefits may have on the economy is if members of this administration start collecting them.

Meanwhile, the administration made its mark in the history of capitalism—in addition to the economies of mass production and mass consumption they created the economy of mass welfare.

The supporters of Keynesian Economics theory, led by Paul Krugman, are trying to convince the country that the reason the economy did not recover is that the previous 800 Billion dollar stimulus package was not big enough. They complain that government involvement in the current economic crisis was insufficient and are calling for another ever greater stimulus package plus broad government involvement in the economy. At this juncture I need to explain how the stimulus works.

I will make it simple so even the Nobel Laureates can understand. Perhaps you remember this math problem that we all studied in school: Water is pumped into the tank and at the same time water is drained from the tank. Depending on the rate of water pumped and drained, the level of water in the tank fluctuates and eventually establishes equilibrium. Capitalism should work the same way. However, if somebody punches a huge hole in the tank's bottom the incoming water will not be able to balance the outgoing flow.

That's exactly what had happened with our economy. The President and Congress have made a huge hole in the country's money tank and everybody was sucking the goodies from it. The revenues could not balance the spending flow and the financial tank went dry.

Instead of closing the hole we are hearing that if we pump more money into the tank (our money which they persist in calling "Stimulus Packages"), there will be sufficient inflow to the tank to balance the outflow, and a level of stability and even prosperity will be restored. What they refuse to recognize is that even if we tax all the rich, as the President suggests, even up to 100% of their income we will not get sufficient inflow to overcome the outflow. Besides, the number of suckers will also rise.

Making matters worse, the money has to come from somewhere—in this case, the administration's money would be borrowed, adding a huge sum to the federal deficit. And that is in the face of extremely low interest rates and a private sector sitting on two trillion dollars of cash. There is obviously no lack of liquidity in the economy. There is something obscene in this picture.

Ironically, this liberal socialist administration and the liberal economists that develop economic policies for the President, suffer from conservatism—conservatism of thinking.

They are all fixated on solving problems; the housing meltdown, the economic downturn, unemployment, instead of understanding the source of the problems and focusing on new opportunities. In order to move forward one has to look forward. Unfortunately, the President and his advisers are looking in an economic rear-view mirror at the economy of mass consumption. Subsequently, the economists and political pundits erroneously believe this economy can be stimulated by consumer spending.

The most recent period of economic growth was fuelled by a massive expansion of credit, which temporarily took the economy beyond its limits. Consumers have already spent more than they could afford through excessive borrowing and cannot spend anymore despite the rock bottom interest rates. At this point, the consumer is broke, the government is broke, the country is broke, and hence we cannot spend our way out of this crisis.

Yet this administration continues to insist that since private enterprises are not investing, the government should invest in the country's infrastructure to stimulate the economy. That is a gross misconception of contemporary capitalism. As I stated earlier, according to the government, US corporations have accumulated cash totaling about two trillion dollars on their balance sheets and they are anxious to invest it. But the President's inconsistent and generally anti-business political atmosphere, compounded by uncertainties and unpredictability of the government tax, health care and environmental regulations, have created an unacceptably high risk business environment. Furthermore, the President is trying to impose government control over the economy and piling up even more regulations on businesses to make them more responsible to the government regulators. As Isaac Newton discovered, "for every action there is·an equal and opposite reaction."

*What the Obama administration and its financial
advisers have failed to understand is that private enterprises defy regulation and refuse to endure permanent
submission to the government authority by with-
holding investment and therefore impede the expansion
of the economy.*

Some of the great American corporations have chosen
to leave this country altogether; leading the exodus are
Foster Wheeler, Tyco, Halliburton, Cooper Industries, Trans-
ocean, Ingersoll-Rand, Noble Drilling, Global Crossing,
Nobous Industries and Seagate Technology, all of whom
are no longer US companies.

Businesses do not take unknown risks. It is as simple
as that.

New Frontiers

It is becoming exceedingly clear that the era of mass
consumption is approaching its end and America is witn-
essing the dawn of a new era in capitalism. This new form
of capitalism will rise from the ashes of this recession like a
phoenix, vibrant and strong, to ignite another economic
boom that will last until the next bust.

Nobody is smart enough to predict what this new
form might be, but a host of very significant developments
in the capitalist system has occurred over the last twenty to
thirty years.

What distinguishes this era from others is the enormous amount of money that has been accumulated by private investment funds and corporations. American corporations have the highest cash levels ever. Apple alone is sitting on around $100 billion in cash. That state of affairs sets up some interesting dynamics.

Until recently only the government could handle projects on the scale of the Hoover Dam and the Interstate Highway System. At present, however, large corporations and investment funds have sufficient resources to build projects on any scale.

Following their capitalist nature, they are looking for returns and there are a few alternatives that offer reasonable margins and acceptable risks. Their options are mostly limited to dividend increases and buyouts of other companies. But consolidation has its limits and dividend increases do little for economic growth.

One area where the opportunities are abundant is the country's decaying infrastructure. It needs repair and expansion. That entire sector of the economy would provide a steady income, good margins, and offer growth with low risk. What a fabulous place to park your money. This is one area on which we all would agree with the President, who has been consistently advocating rebuilding the country's infrastructure.

Our disagreement is over who is going to pay for it. There is no imperative for the government federal, local or otherwise to finance and maintain modern infrastructure when private capital is available.

The challenge of our time is to lift the economy from

stagnation and to put this country onto the path of accelerating growth. It requires opening a new frontier for
economic expansion. Although, conservatives consistently
advocate for small government, and, I belong to this crowd,
it does not mean that small government cannot think big.
Really big, on a massive scale. The US government in the
past has been very successful at exercising its power and
authority to facilitate new frontiers for capitalism creating
long term economic expansion of a colossal magnitude. The
most prominent acts of legislation that left permanent
marks on this country are The Pacific Railroad Act and The
Homestead Act signed by President Lincoln and The
National Interstate and Defense Highways Act signed by
President Dwight D. Eisenhower.

The Homestead Act stimulated settlement of the West.
The Pacific Railroad Act created a new industry and had a
major impact on the development of capitalism in this
country. The importance of building the Interstate Highway system cannot be over emphasized. It is time to take a
bold step into the future.

This task has three principal components. They are
interconnected and interdependent.

1. Privatization of Government Assets

Privatization of government assets could fall under the
category of "massive" and be on the same scale as the
above mentioned initiatives but would not require government funding.

Privatization of the infrastructure which includes, but is not limited to, roads, bridges, tunnels, treatment facilities and government land, would open a new frontier for investment and relieve the federal and local-level governments from the funding, administration, construction, and operation of the infrastructure and would undoubtedly result in greater efficiency, smaller government and lower taxes. But most importantly it will ignite a huge economic boom and offer long-term productive employment to millions of people.

To ensure compliance with the relevant laws and regulations, privately owned roads, bridges, treatment plants and other infrastructure can be regulated like public utilities. This new government-private enterprise relationship would also result in a reduction of the deficit.

Attracting investments for infrastructure would require getting rid of regulations that impede investment and economic development in this country. Just as Republicans advocate tax code simplification, the abolishment or redesign of healthcare legislation, and the restraining of the EPA, it would also require simplification of the process for obtaining permits and the enactment of new laws to provide long-term certainty regarding environmental restrictions and taxation of the assets.

2. Regain Energy Independence

Those of us who have been educated in engineering (not in law or performance art) recognize the undeniable fact that we still live in the nuclear/hydrocarbon age, and that, as I made abundantly clear in an earlier chapter, there is no commercially viable energy alternative to power the sixteen-trillion-dollar economy. The prosperity of this nation demands that we reclaim our energy independence.

As legendary Sheikh Yamani, former OPEC oil minister, said, "The Stone Age didn't end because we ran out of stones and the Hydrocarbon Age will not end because we ran out of oil." There's no doubt that a time will come when these energies are obsolete. But until then we must regain control over our destiny. A sustained, long-term program is needed to drill for oil and to utilize all energy resources available including nuclear energy.

America enjoys enormous energy resources along with the competence and development capabilities available through its energy companies. We should stop referring to Exxon/Mobil, Chevron and the like as oil companies. They are diversified energy companies and ensuring sufficient energy supply is their business. They will develop and produce the most efficient energy type for the nation's consumption just as they have done over the last hundred years.

Without a cheap and reliable energy supply, the country will face profound and insidious vulnerabilities and a sense of impotence will be a prevailing factor in American industrial policies and international relations for years to come.

3. Redefine Free Trade

A popular fallacy promulgated by the Republican and Democratic administrations is so-called free trade. We should realize that there is no such thing as free, whether it is trade or anything else.

In this world economy where technology is available for anyone willing to pay for it, America cannot compete against a world of developing nations. Saying that an American worker is "the most productive in the world" makes for good rhetoric but has little to do with reality. If Chinese enterprises employing the most advanced technologies in the world, do not have to comply with US-style environmental and health regulations, and pay their workers in a day what their American counterparts are making in an hour, this country cannot possibly compete.

American companies looking for higher returns, and in many instances survival, are forced to move jobs overseas.

American trade partners should not expect to reap the benefits of trade that takes advantage of American regulations and high American wages.

None of these objectives above can be achieved in isolation. We must succeed in all three or we will not succeed at all.

American pragmatism shall prevail. To do so, the Democrats and Republicans must overcome their respective ideological zeal and work together to facilitate the opening of a new frontier for capitalism.

The Role of Government

I cannot help but be reminded of the story about the 17th century French businessman Le Gendre who, when asked by then-famous finance minister Colbert how the government can help business, responded, "Laissez-nous faire" — literally "Leave us be." Or, perhaps in plain English, "Leave us alone." That was how the theory of "Laissez faire" capitalism was born. Over the centuries it has proved to be the best tool for unlashing human ingenuity. In the United States where government oppression of private enterprise is relatively feeble compared to the rest of the world, prosperity and human ingenuity flourish, creating the Internet, and such companies as Google, Microsoft, and Apple to name just a few.

A couple of years ago I saw a big headline in the London Times, "Why we don't have our own Bill Gates?" The answer is obvious — in America "Laissez faire" capitalism is not dead.

Yet during this same period, our government has demonstrated that it may save us from fires, epidemics and even Islamic terrorists but cannot save us from our own stupidity. Government itself has become the epitome of stupidity.

Be that as it may, there are things that government can do to limit the impact of a recession and open new frontiers for economic expansion.

First, government can and should enforce bankruptcy laws so that failed enterprises can exit the marketplace in an orderly manner. There is no reason to prop up the dead-wood of our economy.

Second, government can reduce taxes to stimulate investment by big business and increase the public purchasing power so the supply-demand inventory balance can be worked out sooner rather than later. To do that, they need to create real budgets—with stated and planned-for contingencies as well as performance and budget-based incentives.

Third, just as private enterprises cut out fat and got leaner and meaner during the recession, government should use the opportunity to eliminate or reduce some of its bureaucracy and review its regulations to eliminate redundancies and regulations that have a detrimental effect on the economy. This is obviously politically difficult for any government as it increases unemployment.

My suggestion: Create a new government agency, The Department of Deregulation. The department shall review existing regulations every 10 years for the purpose of simplification or deletion of outdated regulations or regulations that proved to be ineffective or detrimental to the economy and to abolish those government agencies that have outlived their usefulness.

What is to be Done

We must stop building the economies of other nations around the world. Saudi Arabia, Kuwait, Arab Emirates are all built with American oil money. China's economy has become a manufacturing plant for American corporations. Profits from the manufacturing goods sold on the American market have built China's economy. It is the time we get wise and re-create the business environment conducive to capitalism in the USA to re-build this country.

The solution to our problems is simple: "Laissez-nous faire." Just let capitalism work.

Chapter Seven

The Road to Our not-so-Bright Future

I Saw the Future and it Does not Work

What is Socialism Anyway?

Socialism is a political philosophy and economic system which promotes egalitarianism—a theory of economic equality. Modern socialism originated in the 18th-century as a working class economic and political movement that opposed private property and criticized the effects of industrialization on society.

In the early 19th-century, "socialism" became a panacea for all the ills of society: Economic, social and political. By the early 20th Century, many socialists became strong advocates of the Soviet model of Marxist-Leninist Socialism for Western Europe and the United States, including the creation of a centrally planned command and control economy. These socialists formed Communist parties in each of their respective countries.

Lenin defined socialism as *"from each according to his abilities and to each according to his contribution."*

"Each according to his contribution" sounds like capitalism, doesn't it? If you work hard, if you are smart, entrepreneurial or you have been blessed with talent you make a greater contribution to society, and you subsequently get a greater reward. So what is the difference? The difference is in each society's assessment of the intrinsic value of an individual's contribution to that society. In the capitalist system value is defined by free market forces and therefore is objective and unlimited.

Capitalism offers an individual economic freedom to work, invent, succeed, and to prosper without limits.

In Socialism, on the other hand, the value of an individual's contribution is defined by the society (government) using Karl Marx's concept that the "universal measure for value, expressed in terms of money, corresponds to the amount of labor time that goes into the making of each commodity." In this case value is subjective and restricted by society, or in this case, by the government that has the power and authority to define what is fair and adequate. Unlike capitalism that is based on individualism, socialism is based on collectivism.

In order for Marxism to work, those who have the greatest abilities and those who work the hardest must be satisfied with the same rewards as those with lesser abilities and those who don't work at all. That is the fundamental difference. According to Marxist orthodoxy, socialism is the lower stage of communism, which is based on the principle of *"from each according to his ability, to each according to his need."* It implies that a person of limited abilities may have unlimited need.

This is a fatal delusion of believers of communism. Remember what Lenin said, "must be neither rich nor poor," the need is defined by the society (government). For example, in the Soviet Union, the eligibility threshold for a new apartment was limited to 100 sq. ft. per person. Therefore, a family of four was eligible for 400 sq. foot of living space. It did not include kitchen, bathroom and other non-living spaces. That is how "to each according to his need" works in a real working people's paradise.

According to Marxist teaching, the upper stage, communism, is only possible after the Socialist stage achieves a level of productivity that ensures an abundance of goods and services sufficient to satisfy all available demand. Again, what is "sufficient" is defined by society.

The supporters of socialism defend it primarily on moral grounds. Their contention assumes that if all people were born equal they should have an equal share of society's wealth.

The obvious fallacy is that people are born with equal rights, not with equal abilities. Equal rights are no guarantee of equal results. Therefore any attempt to create economic equality, such as between the labor of Thomas Edison and a lawn mower is nothing less than a veritable absurdity. Equality is like a horizon, an imaginable line that gets further away as one gets closer. The Soviets tried to reach the horizon of equality but there were always some more equal than others.

The government command and control economy is even worse. It ensures full employment via the distribution of wealth, but doing so de-incentivizes innovation and effectively suppresses growth and productivity. It is nothing more than a modern form of slavery or serfdom. Since all means of production belong to the State, all employees work for the State and, effectively, are property of the State. They are paid in accordance with "their needs," which is not much. They cannot sell their labor on the open market. Now, it becomes easy to see why there is no unemployment in a socialist State. Slaves cannot be unemployed.

The phenomenon was vividly demonstrated in the Soviet Union and other socialist countries.

Regardless of which version of socialism has been tried, whether it was the Dictatorship of the Proletariat or Democratic Socialism Western-style, they all proved to be a colossal failure.

In any event, we are not here to debate the philosophical validity of socialism. History has issued its verdict. The lessons of the past century serve as a reminder that socialism and government control of the economy are not the answer for an ever-changing industrial society.

The contemporary supporters of social justice cannot be persuaded by the lessons of history. The ideas of these people—socialists, liberals, progressives, communists, or Bolsheviks are not new and have been tried quite a few times with horrible consequences. What greatly exacerbated those outcomes was the fact that, contrary to popular belief, liberalism, the ideological basis for all the above labels, is not a social science, but a religion.

Liberals, for the most part, are religious fanatics. They cannot accept an argument. There is no sacrifice too big and no price too high to pay for achieving their ultimate objective—the creation of an egalitarian society.

The difference is that science requires a proof, whether by conducting an experiment, knowledge gained through experience, or historical precedents. Religion, on the other hand is a suspension of critical reason, it requires none of that. Religion is just a set of beliefs.

I once discussed this issue with a KGB General whom I befriended during my long emigration ordeal from the former Soviet Union. I pointed out to him that the great Russian experiment with socialism had failed despite the heavy price tag—economic decline and 30 million victims executed during the process of building the new society. His answer was, "Yes, we made mistakes, we just executed the wrong people." He would not hesitate to start over again, he told me, because this time he knew who the "right" people to execute were.

Americans fare no better. When I came to America, some people seriously asked me why I left a paradise where citizens get free housing, free education and free medical treatment. When I tried to describe to them the horrors and absurdities of socialism they would sigh and politely tell me that Karl Marx's ideas were right, but the implementation was wrong. And at the end of our conversation my interlocutor would often say: "I could do it differently, I would know better..."

As we pointed out earlier, there are different versions of socialism and different strategies for achieving their egalitarian objectives. We have to be mindful, that every ism; communism, socialism or Obamanism, has its supporters and beneficiaries. Hence, we should not be surprised by the populist support Obama is getting while selling his masquerade version of socialism.

Those who imagine themselves on the receiving end,

have every reason to think they will be better off under socialism. We may even see the headline in the American version of "Pravda", the New York Times, declaring, "America without Capitalism: For Most, a Better Life." Ironically, it may be true in the short run, while there is still wealth to be distributed.

All the socialist invocations of the superiority of socialism could not override the reality. As the record shows, despite its populist appeal the system is fundamentally flawed—and has a life expectancy of about 70 years. The Bolshevik revolution took place in Russia in 1917 and totalitarian socialism met its demise in 1986. Western Europe chose the democratic version of socialism in 1945 and seventy years later it is unraveling. North Korean and Cuban totalitarian versions are each in intensive care. Critics of capitalism and inequality failed to recognize two important factors: capitalism is about creating wealth, socialism is about the redistribution of wealth.

The foregoing just confirms Margaret Thatcher's statement that: "The problem with socialism is that eventually you run out of other people's money."

What is Social Justice?

Some people say that Obama is not a socialist; he is a supporter of Social justice. What, then, is Social justice?

The International Labour Organization (ILO), an agency of the United Nations, defines "social justice" as a concept based on "human rights and equality and involves a greater degree of economic egalitarianism through progressive taxation, income redistribution, or even property redistribution."

Furthermore, according to the ILO, "Redistribution of wealth is the transfer of income, wealth or property from some individuals to others caused by a social mechanism such as taxation, monetary policies, welfare or nationalization".

The similarities between the concept of social justice and socialism are so apparent that to anyone who is not hopelessly naïve, social justice is nothing more than socialism in disguise. It is worth pointing out that the ILO is an international body and it is not talking about social justice in any individual country, they talking about world justice and the redistribution of wealth on a worldwide scale. It would not be very difficult to figure out whose wealth they are dreaming of redistributing.

Whether you call it social justice or socialism, the underlying fundamental is building an egalitarian society. Whether it is done by the outright expropriation of property like the Bolsheviks did or it is done through taxation and regulation, the outcome is presumed to be the same. The tactics and methods may vary; but the final objective is a "makeable" society.

"Change will not come if we wait for some other person or some other time. We are the ones we've been waiting for. We are the change that we seek," Barack Obama said. This is a theme he borrowed from the communist anthem "Internationale":

"There are no supreme saviors

Neither God, nor Caesar, nor tribune.

Producers, let us save ourselves!"

Supporters of social justice are trying to camouflage the issue claiming that the moral justification for egalitarianism is deeply embedded in spiritual aspects of our lives and that ethics and social responsibility have a central place in Judaism and Christianity.

It is worth pointing out that religion is separate from the state in this country. In this democratic society, the religious obligation to perform charity and philanthropic acts is not directed by the government. They are symbols of individual goodness cherished in our society. The roots of this goodness have nothing to do with the redistribution of wealth or building egalitarian dreams.

Over the years Socialists of every stripe have been working on the destruction of capitalism with implacable determination. The movement has gone from spectacular triumphs to humiliating defeats. From victory in Russia in 1917 and the conquest of Eastern Europe and China in 1930s and 40s; to what seemed an unstoppable march in Africa and Latin America in the 1960s and 70s; to the spectacular collapse of the Soviet Union, the liberation of Eastern Europe and the economic liberalization of China in the 1980s. Never the less, their efforts in this country and our society have had the same destructive effect as drops of water on a stone. It has over the time eroded our sense of self-reliance and personal responsibility.

Regardless of how these people call themselves: social

justice supporters, socialists, liberals, progressives, Marxists or Bolsheviks; regardless of what lipstick they put on a pig, it is still a Marxist pig.

The 17th Amendment

One of the reasons for the mess this government got us into, is that we have forgotten the principles this country was built upon; and we need to be reminded of the reason for certain provisions in the Constitution that made this country great in the first place.

The US Constitution emanated from the Great Compromise of 1787. It is worth being reminded of what was at stake and the essence of the compromise. At the time, the United States was a union of independent States that were trading some of their independence for the common defense, collective security and general welfare.

The real issue was the preservation of the States' sovereignty against a "tyranny of the majority." The Great Compromise provided the people representation in the House in proportion to the population of each State; while the Senate would represent the interests of sovereign States by being weighted equally between the states.

The House of Representatives was intended to be a "People's House," directly elected by the majority of people in their respective districts. While the Senators were to be selected by the state legislatures to represent the States in retaining their sovereignty.

To make it abundantly clear, the Senate was not

intended to represent the interests of the people, per se. It was intended to represent the interests of the States. The duty of the Senators was to zealously guard the power of the States. In giving elective power to the States, the framers of the Constitution hoped to protect the States' independence. That was then. And, this is how it is now:

In 1913 the Seventeenth Amendment was ratified, providing for the direct election of U.S. senators by citizens of each State. The amendment effectively took power from the states, making a mockery of the original intent of the U.S. Constitution.

The States lost their power and independence.

The Senators, once elected by the people, are no longer bound to the interests of their States; instead they have become committed to their parties' agenda. Just think about it: If we didn't have the 17th Amendment, none of the fighting about Obama Care and many other very important issues, would ever have taken place. The fifty-four senators, representing the twenty-seven States that opposed the legislation, would simply have voted it down.

There is more: With the passage of the 17th Amendment, the Senate lost not only its original intended purpose, it became redundant at best, and an impediment at worst. Among the victims of the 17th Amendment, was the 10th Amendment. The Amendment was originally designed to enforce the principle of Federalism and stated that the powers not granted to the Federal government under the Constitution, nor prohibited by it to the States, are reserved to the States respectively, or to the people.

After ratification of the 17th Amendment, the 10th de facto ceased to exist. Nowadays, be it the Republican or Democratic Party, if the party controls both branches of government it can pass any law they want. States have no say in the proposed legislation, all the more so now, where in a politically polarized environment the Senators vote mostly the party line.

The Third World War

The Third World War has begun and the enemy is not the one we expected. America and the Western world are facing a danger such as it has never faced before. Our enemy is not a government nor is it a country. We are fighting enemies who hate us so much that they are willing to kill themselves in order to kill us. This war puts our conventional Army, Navy and Air forces at a serious disadvantage. There is practically no defense against this kind of warfare.

The enemy is Islam who is waging war against our civilization. Our President and the Left, living in a politically correct universe, insist that acts of terror are perpetrated by extremists. Islam, they say, is a peaceful religion and the majority of Muslims are law-abiding citizens—ignoring the fact that these peaceful citizens were celebrating the 9/11 attack from the West Bank to Jakarta.

The President and his leftist supporters maintain that all cultures are equal and equally deserving of respect and celebration. That may sound noble, but it overlooks the fact that the cradle of freedom and democracy was the Western world, not the land of Islam. Western civilization, governed by reason, discovered science and technology, and has produced culture that the rest of the world relishes. The land of Islam, governed by faith, contributed almost nothing to the advances of science and culture since the development of arithmetic a few thousand years ago.

It does not get any better nowadays. Islam is a culture in which any member of the family can kill a woman for having an affair. As a matter of fact it is the duty of a brother to kill his sister if she dishonors the family. Worse yet, this so-called culture glorifies female mutilation—i.e., cutting a little girl's clitoris with a dirty razor without anesthesia.

The President deliberately ignores those important facts in an attempt to appease Islam. Furthermore, the President who has been a vocal defender of women's rights to have an abortion and free contraceptives is silent on the horrifying treatment of women in the land of Islam.

In his infamous Cairo speech, Mr. Obama actually declared that "I consider it part of my responsibility as President of the United States to fight against negative stereotypes of Islam wherever they appear." The examples above are not the stereotypes he had in mind, they are facts, and about them, he is quiet.

The President, by practicing the politics of appeasement, has a difficult time coming to terms with the teachings of the father of modern terrorism. Vladimir Lenin, who was both a perpetrator of terrorism and on the receiving end of it, taught that, "Terror can be conquered only with greater terror."

That may reveal why the President is not following the teaching of his ideological fathers on this important issue while following them so faithfully in the areas of politics and economics.

The President lacks a coherent strategy in this arena, much as he does in others, which leads to strategic and tactical inconsistencies. In this case, a failure to call our conflict with Islam a war has resulted in wide-spread confusion. On one hand, the President never misses a chance to release captured terrorists back into their environment so they can continue killing. On the other, American drones are killing terrorists with deadly precision in Afghanistan, Yemen and other parts of the world.

At one point, the administration decided to prosecute the Al Qaeda Leaders including Khalid Sheikh Mohammed as civilians in domestic U.S. courts. However, there was a good chance that the terrorists would beat the rap on technicalities, just like Bill Ayers (another terrorist who is also Obama's friend), and walk free. In another instance, the President approved a raid in Pakistan to kill Osama Bin Laden. It seems the President is torn between his sympathies for Islam and the realities of war.

Once again, the President is caught in conflicting currents. He insists that acts of terrorism are a legal issue and must be dealt with by our legal system. Despite the fact that Obama refuses to call this a war, he is sending drones to kill people abroad, in countries such as Pakistan and Yemen (even Americans) without due process.

If this is a war, no American civil or criminal law applies and the President's actions are fully justified. However, if this is not a war, then how can the President execute people, including Americans, without due process? Although, this is not a war, the President, nonetheless, personally chooses the drone "kill" targets, as the New York Times recently revealed. Although deciding who lives and who dies may play well into the President's feeling of eminence; it is neither legal nor does it do much to win a war.

Just like in politics, the President may choose to ignore reality, but he cannot change it. The reality is that we are in a state of a war: the Third World War. In order to win a war, we have to understand the enemy and its objectives. Napoleon once said, "If you do not understand your enemy, you have lost." It should be taken as a warning, in effect, of worse to come.

To say most Muslims are moderates and have nothing to do with the fanatical Islamic terrorists is like saying the Germans were a highly cultured, peaceful people and the mass murder of Jews was perpetrated by National Socialist extremists. There are many striking similarities between Nazi Germany and today's Muslim world, all of which this current government and the Left have chosen to ignore.

The Nazis' doctrine called for supremacy of the Aryan race and the extermination of the Jews. I am sure that the

Left (which has many Jewish supporters) would consider those policies extreme.

However the Left fails to recognize that, like the Nazis' doctrine, the Koran segregates the human race into two groups: Muslims and infidels; and just like the Nazis' doctrine, the Koran calls for the killing of infidels and specifically Jews.

The Muslims' view of the world is that they alone possess absolute knowledge and God-given supreme right over the infidels. In both instances we are dealing with one group of people (if one wants to call them people) who claim superiority over the rest of the human race and seek to have them destroyed or enslaved.

We should make no mistake: Islam is not just a religion but also a political totalitarian movement, just like Communism or Fascism. The movement embraces a fanatical agenda that includes racial supremacy and a Marxist-type utopian/egalitarian standard of virtue. However, unlike Communism or Fascism, which were adopted by countries that could be defeated, Islam is represented by unlimited human resources around the globe that cannot be defeated in strictly military terms.

The Muslims of the world are united in the struggle to provide moral, financial and logistical support to those who are on the front line of war with the infidels. That silent but effective network of support allows terrorists to avoid security forces, survive, plan, recruit new members and provide training.

Working in the Arab world during the last decade, I have met many Muslims that insisted that they had nothing to do with terrorism. The problem is that they remain silent in fear of the so-called extremists. They do not publicly condemn terror; and they continue to donate money to cover organizations that offer moral and financial support to the terrorist movement. They, just like most Germans, do not want to know.

In any event, we should not be confused by this silent minority about the true nature of Islam; just as the world was not confused about the nature of Nazism because of the small anti-fascist movement inside Germany.

We should not be apologetic for judging all of them by the behavior of most of them.

The Left's position on the Muslim threat is inconsistent, immoral and reprehensible. But that should not surprise us: The Left did not consider Hitler extreme at the time, and supported the proposal to nominate Hitler for the Nobel Peace Prize. The Left has always had a natural attraction to totalitarian, bloody regimes. They admired Stalin, Mao, and in more recent times Castro, Che Guevara and Hugo Chavez.

Americans have been in denial of this danger since the early 1970s when the Palestinian Liberation Organization (PLO) began committing terrorist acts against Israelis. To paraphrase German Pastor Martin Niemoller, who was imprisoned in Dachau concentration camp, the world was silent because the victims were Jews and we were not Jews. Even worse, the world encouraged the terrorists by awarding the Nobel Peace Prize to the PLO chief terrorist Yasser Arafat. Since then terrorists have taken to Europe, but we are not Europeans; and Asia, but we are not Asians. The history of terrorism is reminiscent of what Niemoller wrote about the Nazis:

> "In Germany they first came for the communists
> and I didn't speak up because I wasn't a communist.
> They came for the Jews
> and I didn't speak up because I wasn't a Jew.
> Then they came for the trade Unionists
> and I didn't speak up because I wasn't a trade
>   Unionist.
> Then they came for the Catholics
> and I didn't speak up because I was a Protestant.
> Then they came for me and by that time no one was
>   left to speak up."

Today the terrorists are at our doorsteps but the administration still practices appeasement. The President and the mayor of New York, with the support of the Left, are perfectly willing to let the Muslims build their Mosque of Triumph in proximity to the destroyed World Trade Center, just as they built the Al-Aqsa Mosque on the site of the Second Temple in Jerusalem after conquering the city in the seventh century.

In Afghanistan, the President's policies are just as confusing as on the domestic front. The Vice President during an interview with Newsweek told the magazine, "Look, the

Taliban per se is not our enemy. That's critical." Never mind that they are killing Americans and the Taliban cannot name new commanders fast enough, even as they get killed by American drones. If the Taliban is not our enemy, who are our boys and girls fighting? And why are they dying in Afghanistan?

Can anybody make sense of this?

The objective reality is that the world is divided into two types of societies; a society where violence is condemned; and one where violence is glorified. One society built on the foundation of liberty and the pursuit of happiness; and the other which worships violence and death. One society is where success and respect are measured in capital; and another whose virtues are measured in power and violence.

Saddam Hussein once said, 'If you kill a man—you are a murderer; if you kill hundreds—you are a hero; but if you kill thousands—you are a conqueror." This is the mentality of the other society where terror is an instrument of power. Whether it is a war on terror or a war in Iraq or Afghanistan, if we are not prepared to kill thousands, we cannot be respected. Conventional thinking is that democratic civilizations are humanitarians; and that separates us from barbarians. Whether we can do what needs to be done anymore or whether we have just watered down our genes to where we are incompetent and ineffective, history will be the judge.

In the past, civilized society had little hesitation to use all means at its disposal to protect and defend its ideals.

Bombing Dresden in 1945 was a clear act of terror aimed at German civilians to break the Germans' resolve. Dropping two nuclear bombs on Japan was hardly a humanitarian act either. Our contemporary American challenge is not the military aspect of killing a lot of people; it is the moral issue, regardless of reasoning and justification. The undeniable truth is that terror is a weapon of tyrants and terrorism is the enemy of liberty. Whether this nation is prepared to conquer terror with greater terror—remains an open question.

The way we define and articulate American foreign policy toward the Arab world and how we, as a nation, deal with terrorism are interrelated. Although, the purpose of terrorism is to terrorize, a war on terror is not just a psychological assault, it is also a military confrontation and a political matter.

The introduction of Wilsonian principles in the Arab world without understanding the fundamentals of tribal societies has proved disastrous for this country. The goals of building democratic nations in recent U.S. incursions in Iraq and Afghanistan have proved impossible in the face of an Islamic culture that violently rejects Western values. The fallacy that by executing a civil war, we could build a nation and create democratic institutions at the same time has, instead, driven the U.S. into protracted and costly military conflicts with no end in sight.

The task before our nation is to define our interests to shape our commitments; and not allow the existing commitments to define our interests. Once we clearly define our interests and commitments, it will be time for Americans to find out, to paraphrase John F. Kennedy, whether we are free men standing up to our responsibilities and whether The United States has the will to face up to the enemy.

The American challenge is to abandon denial, define the enemies, stop appeasement, face the threat, and use all means at our disposal to grant the ultimate wish to those who proclaim that they love death more that we love life.

Chapter Eight

The Power of Demagoguery and Lies

It Moves Nations

Obama's Biggest Economic Recovery Plan in History or the Biggest Economic Fraud in History

Obama's stimulus packages come in three basic types. In the first, the federal government puts money directly into the hands of consumers. The hope is that consumers will use the money to increase their purchases of goods and services. In the second, the federal government directly purchases goods and services, including infrastructure projects, equipment, software, law enforcement, and education, hoping this activity will increase jobs and spending. In the third, the federal government sends grants to state and local governments in the hope that those governments will use the funds to purchase goods and services, and hire more policemen, firefighters, teachers and generally more government employees.

In this sense when the President says that without the stimulus the unemployment numbers would be higher, he is correct. No doubt about that. It is also true that putting more people on the government payroll to reduce unemployment numbers may be a good political ploy of smoke and mirrors as a short-term solution, but it does not solve long-term economic problems. Actually, it could make them worse. As stimulus money runs out, local governments will be scrambling to find new sources of revenue to keep those firefighters and police offices on the payroll. Local governments will then have little choice but to raise taxes, which would take more money from the economy, thereby exacerbating the ongoing crises.

Hence, when the President says he needs four more years to get this country on the right track, let's see if he can be trusted.

The President said that if we pass the $767 billion stimulus package—that turned out to be $862 billion, just $95 billion more—we would keep unemployment no higher than 8%. One important caveat, in 2009 the official unemployment numbers reflected actual unemployment, but after prolonged periods of economic downturn as people began exhausting their benefits and are no longer registered on federal rosters, the actual number of unemployed is far greater than the official numbers. Experts estimate the current actual unemployment rate is around 15-18%. The administration also promised to create (not save) between three and four million jobs by the end of 2010, 90% in the private sector. That would come at the price of $287 000 and $215 000 per job respectively.

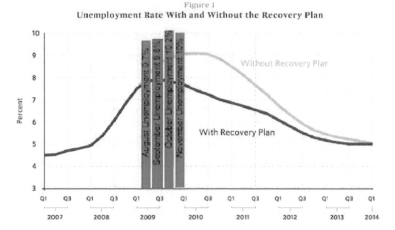

This chart was copied directly from Obama's report, published in January 2009, to persuade us that the "stimulus" or Recovery Plan would prevent millions of layoffs. Obama promised a maximum 8% unemployment rate if the recovery plan passed, or 9.1% without a recovery plan.
We added the red bars showing official unemployment rates.

Figure 1
Unemployment Rate With and Without the Recovery Plan

The money was spent. The result; unemployment has been above 8% during all of Obama's term, the national debt skyrocketed and the economy is still in the toilet. If a strategy does not accomplish the stated objectives, a reasonable observer may conclude that the strategy has failed. Not with this President. He has not finished with America. He asks for more time. I think before we vote on the issue of more time, we want to know why his program did not work. Did the President tell the truth when he made those promises or did he simply not know what he was talking about? The answer is in the January 9, 2009 report, "The Job Impact of the American Recovery and Reinvestment Plan," issued by the President's Council of Economic Advisers. The report stated:

"It should be understood that all of the estimates presented in this memo are subject to significant margins of error," the report states. "There is more fundamental uncertainty that comes with any estimate of the effects of a program. Our estimates of economic relationships and rules of thumb are derived from historical experience and so will not apply exactly in any given episode. Furthermore, the uncertainty is surely higher than normal now because the current recession is unusual both in its fundamental causes and its severity."

In plain English, the administration had no clue what they were projecting and probably did not care. The probability to win in roulette when betting on red or black is 50% (47.4% in American roulette because of the green 00). The probability of winning in the President's roulette was probably even lower. This whole report is nothing more than an exercise in intellectual futility. The discussion whether the stimulus worked is strictly academic: as I ascertained earlier, the main purpose for the stimulus was to spend money. In this sense it did work.

Capacity versus Demand

The President claims that the economy is moving in the right direction because instead of losing 700 000 jobs per month as we did in 2009 when he took office, the economy has been creating 200 000 jobs per month for the last twenty months. He credits this to his stewardship and the stimulus package.

The economic truth is that it proves exactly the opposite. As we established earlier the sources of economic downturns are overproduction and overcapacity. At the beginning of a crisis the economy shrinks and excess of capacity causes the labor force to be reduced to meet diminishing demand. However, just like the stock market, in a panic too much capacity gets liquidated and the labor market underestimates the need.

The meager job growth during this prolonged period of time is merely evidence that capacity finally got in line with demand but the economy is not growing. It also indicates that the stimulus had no effect on the job market. We remain in a state of prolonged economic stagnation.

They are Ignorant. But They Vote

In a previous chapter, I asked a question that many Americans such as myself, who are in a state of disbelief, would like answered: "How did a man with no experience at anything, who is intellectually shallow, and has no record of accomplishment in any field, propel himself in so short a time, into the Presidency of the United States?"

Obama appeared at the right time. Lack of education and historical perspective, together with a proliferation of political illiteracy on the background of the impending economic crisis created fertile ground for a talented demagogue to seduce the nation.

A weak candidacy on the Republican side also helped.

However, the 2008 elections were not just Barack Obama's personal achievement but also a historic victory for the so-called Progressive movement in this country.

For the last 50 years, the progressives have been waging an all-out war against American institutions such as education, religion, and family values. Their tireless efforts have paid off. Early on, they realized that there is no better way to subvert America than to have a degraded education system.

The effect on education cannot be underemphasized. "Give me four years to teach the children" Lenin said, "and the seed I have sown will never be uprooted."

Back in 1983, the Reagan administration published, "A Nation at Risk: The Imperative of Education Reform." The report warned that the decay of American schools was becoming a threat to the very survival of the country. But, the very powerful combination of teachers' unions, state bureaucracies, and the democratic establishment, defeated the initiative.

Ironically, it was the Civil Rights movement of the 1960s that subverted the system by offering equal opportunity in education and in employment.

As usual, the Left confused equality of opportunities with equality of results.

Integrated schools were supposed to provide quality education for all citizens regardless of color. In reality, there were large gaps between the education, behavior and performance of white and black children. Instead of recognizing these differences, enforcing discipline, and providing black children with additional help and assistance, the schools geared their curriculum and educational standards to the lowest common denominator. Doing so, they indeed did produce an equality of results: equality in illiteracy.

These newly integrated schools became factories of illiteracy producing inferior students year after year. That was in stark contrast with the rest of the world. The rest of the world, particularly the Soviet Union and China realized the importance of education in modern economies, which were becoming more complex and knowledge-intensive than in the past. The rise of China and the decline of the United States can be traced directly to the quality of education.

When I started thinking about the importance of

education, I recalled my first day of school in the Soviet Union. The principal made clear in words I will never forget, the educational values she expected of seven year olds. "Children," she said, "No one will get out of here illiterate; those who want to learn, we will teach you; those who do not want to learn, we will force you." I still feel the chill of her words in my spine.

We are not here to debate or make suggestions about the American educational system. The American educational system has been a disgrace for many years, producing an illiterate electorate that gravely endangers our democracy.

In order to become a U.S. citizen, one must demonstrate a basic level of civic knowledge. Not so if you are a US born citizen. According to a recently released Gallup/ Harris poll, a full 37% of American citizens are incapable of identifying their home state on a map of the United States. 22% think this is "a place to definitely explore when I finally get my passport."

It should come as no surprise if some are proud that America defeated Hitler during the Vietnam War in Iraq.

They are so ignorant, it is frightening. But they vote.

Now we can appreciate the Founding Fathers' apprehension about the American public as expressed in some of the statements from the Constitutional Convention of 1787. Here is one expressed by Delegate Gerry, "The people are uninformed, and would be misled by a few designing men."

And another, by delegate Mason: "The extent of the

country renders it impossible that the people can have the requisite capacity to judge of the respective pretensions of the candidates."

By 2008 the American electorate was well prepared for CHANGE.

We can debate the numbers produced by the Department of Education or the United Nations demonstrating the deplorable state of American education. I do not think the numbers tell the story.

I had firsthand experience with the American education system in the mid-1970s when as a result of Jewish emigration from the Soviet Union, Russian emigrants started sending their kids to public school here. Children who were in 6th and 7th grade in the USSR were tested and accepted, despite poor English, into the 8th and 9th grade. By the 1990s, the situation was getting progressively worse.

The story of one exchange student from Kazakhstan reveals the depth of the problem in very personal terms.

In 1995, I was working for an international Engineering and Construction Company in Houston. We used to do a lot of work in Kazakhstan, one of the former Soviet Republics. In the course of our work, I established a very good relationship with the Deputy Minister of Energy.

His daughter, Irina, was a straight "A" student in Almaty which at the time was the capital of Kazakhstan. She won the privilege of becoming an exchange student and was invited to spend a year in an American school. This was considered quite an honor. The girl had just finished

9th grade and was accepted to the 10th grade for the following school year.

She arrived in Wichita, Kansas, where she was met by an American family. She stayed in their home and was well taken care of. A few weeks later, her father called me, sounding desperate. "Alex," he said, "Irina was assigned to a class for mentally retarded kids. Please help me transfer her to a regular class. Please explain to them that she is a bright girl. She just has a poor command of English."

Of course, I immediately understood what was going on. I should have warned him about American schools, but he was so proud that his daughter had been awarded a spot in the exchange program that I just couldn't bring myself to tell him before.

"Boris," I said, "Irina is not in a class for the mentally retarded. That's just what a typical American class is like." He was shocked.

"Alex," he pleaded, "You have to help me. She's a tenth grader. What they are teaching her, she learned in the sixth grade. When she comes back home she will never be able to graduate." he said.

Fortunately, my employer was headquartered in Kansas and many executives had friends and relatives in Wichita. One of company's vice presidents knew a dean of Wichita University and asked him to intervene. After an interview, the girl was allowed to take courses at the university. The story has a happy ending. This young lady graduated with honors, got married, and today lives happily in the United States. I can't help but wonder, if she had

children, would she send them to an American public
school?

The Jewish Question

I have been fascinated and perplexed by those Jewish-
Americans who voted for Obama in 2008.

It seems like the choice was clear and unambiguous.
On the Republican side was a war hero, a strong supporter
of Israel, an experienced politician with a strong track
record and commitment to public service. On the other
side, for the Democrats, was a young man of Muslim background, an inexperienced politician with no track record of
accomplishment whose personal files were sealed. Moreover, this man had dubious connections with anti-Semites
and American-haters.

I have asked "Why?" so many times, of so many Jews.
The question is entirely legitimate given that Jews are over-
whelmingly liberal as well as being disproportionately left
of liberal. The best answer I received was, "I did not vote
for him, but I am not going to vote for him this time." You
ask a Jewish question, you get a Jewish answer.

As prominent Zionist Zev Jabotinsky once said, "Logic
is an art of the Greeks; a Jew has his own logic." Jewish
logic is the logic of catastrophe. Jews do not detect danger;
they face it when it comes. A Jew will ignore the weather
forecast and forego buying an umbrella. He will get wet
and contract pneumonia first, and then tell you that as he
has already survived pneumonia, the umbrella can wait.

The old saw that, "There are two types of Jews—those who believe that Judaism is about social justice and those who know Hebrew," contains more than a kernel of truth. By and large, orthodox Jews voted for McCain.

Social justice is deeply embedded in Judaism; and many Jews believe that the only way to achieve a just society is through leftist policies.

The problem is that their religion is not Judaism; it is almost every other possible "ism," (with the exceptions of conservatism and Fascism) such as liberalism, socialism, feminism, environmentalism and Marxism.

Speaking of which, the 1917 Bolshevik revolution in Russia that brought so much suffering to the people of Russia, including Jews, was, in fact, a Jewish revolution. Based on socialist theories developed by a Jewish philosopher and economist, Karl Marx, the principal inspiration, organization and the driving power of the revolution came from Jewish leaders such as Trotsky (Bronstein), Zinoviev (Apelbaum), Kamenev (Rosenfeldt), Sverdlov (Rubenstine) Larine, Uritsky, Steclov (Nakhamkes) all of whom later assumed major positions in Lenin's government. Most of them changed their Jewish names to Russian ones. In effect, Jews founded and shaped the Soviet State. Yet these same Jewish Bolsheviks quickly became the first victims of the Soviet State. By 1937 practically all of them had become victims of Stalin's terror, executed, or murdered abroad like Leon Trotsky. Still they would not abandon their love for socialism.

In the late 1920s, German Jews voted for Hitler's

National Socialist Party, only to become victims of the
Holocaust a decade later. They chose to ignore Hitler's
anti-Semitic rhetoric believing that it was merely for
domestic consumption. They doubted Hitler could be bad;
after all, he was a socialist.

The Jewish love affair with socialism that began in
Russia, continued in Germany, and endures today in
America. An examination of the current socialist Obama
government reveals a similar Jewish pattern. Living in
ghettos for two millennia, the Jewish people have been
struggling to reconcile their tragic history with the logic of
contemporary reality. They have a difficult time coming to
terms with the freedom and equal opportunities that
America offers. They continue to fight for social justice
refusing to realize that, as far as Jews are concerned, they
have accomplished it in this country well beyond their
wildest expectations. Sons and daughters of the first immigrants who dug trenches and washed dishes in New
York became doctors, lawyers, senators, bankers and
industrialists.

Unfortunately, the descendants of the first immigrants
inherited the genetic memories of their ghetto ancestors.
They feel guilty for their success; they feel guilty for achieving a standard of living in many instances better than the
indigenous population. They are constantly seeking forgiveness for their own survival. They are prisoners of their
own insecurity. Their guilt at their own success has led
them to take on the cause of every underdog and liberal
movement, no matter how deserving, no matter how

rational, no matter whether it is in their best interest or self-preservation. Over the last century, no group has more consistently voted against their interest. A dubious honor, at best.

Socialism, which began with the fanaticism of grand-parents, has been transformed into fear of parents and subsequently to the habits of children and grandchildren, is deeply embedded in the Jewish DNA.

Jews continue to disregard the teachings of their fellow member of the tribe, Karl Marx, that socialism is about redistribution. Redistribution means taking from one group of citizens and giving it to others. Bolsheviks took from the bourgeoisie; Nazis took from the Jews. The contemporary American Neo-Bolsheviks would like to take from the rich; even though there are many Jews among them.

Recently, I was in a Las Vegas restaurant with some of my Jewish friends, talking politics over dinner. At the table behind ours was another Jewish gathering who overhead our conversation. One of them turned around asked one of my friends if he really was going to vote for Romney. My friend replied that he will vote for a cock roach if it runs against Obama. Perhaps, there is a glimmer of hope that this time the Jews will get out of their intellectual ghetto and start voting based on logic not habits.

No Representation Without Taxation

The slogan of the original Tea Party was "No taxation without representation." At the time, they were objecting to being taxed and not having a say in their governance. Today, we face a different and more subtle problem: *"Representation without taxation."*

Currently, approximately 50% of Americans do not pay income tax, instead they are voting to spend other people's money. The Democratic Party has successfully corralled these voters with promises of a better life, free health care for all, better job benefits for workers, stronger unions, and a government that will pass laws to pay for all of this out of our own treasury.

Remember Thomas Jefferson said, "A democracy is nothing more than mob rule, where fifty-one percent of the people may take away the rights of the other forty-nine." Thomas Jefferson pointed out the problem facing modern America: We have more people voting for a living than people working for a living.

The United States is beginning to look more and more like the Roman Empire around the second century CE. By that time the Empire had begun to unravel from within. The city of Rome had become a welfare state. Free food was handed out daily. The agrarian economy that used to be the foundation of the State was falling apart, unable to compete with cheaper crops imported from North Africa. Just like North Africa's cheap crop was destroying Rome's agriculture, cheap Chinese imports are destroying America's industries. The United States, just like the Roman Empire, has become a welfare state.

Obama's Re-election Strategy

Ironically, Change itself is a contradiction between Obama's policies of wealth distribution and job creation, which according to the political gurus, is critical to the President's reelection.

Conventional wisdom is that in order to get reelected, the President needs to get the economy going and reduce unemployment, but his anti-capitalist agenda is in conflict with the law of economics. Obama's unrestrained spending, high taxation, government regulation of industry and financial services, are effectively impeding any significant expansion of the economy.

Political pundits would say that it makes no sense for the President to continue policies that stall the recovery, result in higher unemployment, and subsequently hamper his reelection prospects. I beg to differ. As I said earlier, the President is not governed by conventional wisdom.

To understand the President one has to get into the mind of a Bolshevik. The President's interest in the economy is limited to its impact on his reelection campaign. No more, no less.

On the surface, the President is facing an awkward task reconciling the irreconcilable. In reality, the President does not need a good economy to get reelected; all he needs are good economic numbers. Since his administration is producing the numbers and sometimes the numbers get adjusted in subsequent reports, this political high-wire act may not be a "mission impossible." Moreover, the political gurus underestimate the Bolsheviks' sinister strategy.

The President's strategy is to get reelected not in spite of the bad economy but because of it.

The cornerstone of Obama's reelection strategy is not an improved economy but increased dependency. A bad economy justifies the expansion of entitlements and the proliferation of dependency. The President skillfully uses the economic crisis to shore up his base. Millions of Americans depend on the government one way or the other. They are Obama's army.

In a sense, Obama is taking a page from FDR's playbook and Lenin's teachings. FDR successfully exploited economic difficulties to appoint himself President for life. Roosevelt's formula of tax, spend (buy votes), and get elected proved to be unbeatable. Democrats controlled the House for 60 years and there is a good chance they will control it for another 60 years.

There is one more not so subtle difference. FDR's America was a country of predominantly self-sufficient individuals who were not used to and did not live off government handouts. Hence at the end of FDR's tenure, America was ready and willing to go back to free markets and could easily abandon the idea of "regulated" capitalism that FDR may have introduced.

As we discussed earlier, today about 50% of Americans don't pay any income tax, and millions are receiving welfare checks, food stamps and other forms of government assistance.

All Obama needs to do is to increase this by a few percentage points to put this country in an irreversible decline. Expanding government programs like welfare, food stamps, free health care, and student loan forgiveness will do just that. His task is quite easier than FDR's. It may sound cynical, but maintaining a crisis and effectively exploiting it does serve the President's reelection strategy.

In this respect the President uses the experience of his infamous predecessors. Lenin was a master of taking advantage of upheavals. He believed that crises create opportunities for change, or, in his mind, a revolution. "Our task," wrote Lenin in 1902 in 'What Is to Be Done,' "is to utilize every manifestation of discontent, and to collect and utilize every grain of rudimentary protest."

Taking advantage of a crisis has always been a strategy for extremists to make fundamental changes in society. In recent history, the Bolsheviks skillfully used the war and the economic downturn in Russia to overthrow the Democratic Provisional Government in 1917 and impose a dictatorship of the proletariat; or consider the 1930 Reichstag election, where the Nazis took advantage of Germany's economic and political crisis to gain 143 seats — a vast improvement on their previous showing — which led to the demise of the Weimar Republic. A senior Nazi official, Gregor Strasser, claimed that what was a disaster for Weimar was "good, very good for us."

"Never allow a crisis to go to waste," White House

Chief of Staff Rahm Emanuel told the New York Times echoing Lenin and Strasser, "There are opportunities to do big things," Emanuel said.

This administration was shamelessly excited about an opportunity to exploit a national emergency to push for CHANGE in 2008, and there is no reason to alter this winning strategy for the coming elections other than to substitute FORWARD for Change.

Over the years the Democrats have built armies of supporters and a diversified arsenal of election weaponry.

Government employees are one of the many divisions of Obama's army. Obama has greatly expanded this army in the last three years and increased their pay scale. Nearly 3 million Americans—or roughly 2% of the U.S. Labor Force—are employed in more than 800 occupations for more than 100 Federal government agencies! An additional 5 million Americans work for State governments and 14 million Americans are employed by local governments. That's a total of 22 million Americans—14% of the Labor Force—employed at the local, State and Federal levels.

Let's not forget the elderly. As many as 61 million of Americans are collecting Social Security and Social Supplementary Income (SSI). Most of these people don't care about Social security going broke. It has been going broke for decades. They just want to get their checks, and feel comfortable that there will be enough Social Security for their lifetime. Any talk about prospective changes, modifications or improvements raises their anxiety. They will most likely vote for the status quo.

These strategic advantages for the Democrats will be augmented with the most destructive weapon in Obama's arsenal; demagoguery and lies. The President offers a very powerful message to the country: that while millions of people are suffering, the millionaires and billionaires enjoy lower tax rates, pocketing "money they do not need." Since Obama has already decided for them that they do not need their money, as the reasoning goes we should invest more money in more food stamps or solar energy.

While advancing CHANGE, Democrats will argue that high unemployment is not Obama's fault. It is George Bush's. Furthermore, the Republicans want to cut the duration of unemployment benefits and make millions of American suffer. Third, the Republicans will reform entitlements and deprive grandma of Medicare and poor children of food stamps. And finally, the Republicans will make everybody pay some income tax (raise taxes) while preserving low taxes for the rich.

These are some of the very compelling reasons for those who enjoy "Representation without Taxation" to re-elect Comrade Obama.

This segment of the population is happy to have Obama make us "who are unequally rich, equally poor" as Fox News political analyst Brit Hume put it. This may explain why even in an economy with an unlimited deficit, where jobs have ground to a halt and the future is bleak, the President still enjoys a 47% approval rating.

Will CNN be "keeping them honest"? I would not hold my breath. The media, whose opposition to the

Republicans is a permanent part of the political landscape, will take pride in unmercifully attacking honorable men who genuinely dissent from the President's views and policies. They will try to move the political discourse from debating policies to recycling the smears, demagoguery, and distortions brought on by the Democrats, with no sense of proportion.

What lies will the Democrats in partnership with the media promulgate? Will we learn that Romney had a hit and run accident in which an old black woman was killed or that his secret bank account in the Virgin Islands has been used to finance drug dealers, or that his request for an Israeli passport was turned down despite the fact that his great-grandmother was Jewish? In this manner, no lie will be too big to tell and no promise too outrageous to promote.

The press will not find it distasteful to replace the ancient Roman tenet, "Asserted without proof, shall be denied without proof" with Lenin's rule, "*A lie told often enough becomes the truth.*"

The strategy of class warfare and the use of dependency that the President is engaging in, worked for the Bolsheviks in the past; and there is no reason to believe it will not work this time.

In any event, we have to give the President credit where credit is due; the scheme is resourceful and takes a lot of guts to implement.

Epilogue

The Enemies Are at the Gates

¡No pasaran!

While walking among some Greek and Roman ruins with my daughter, I experienced a mixture of melancholy and deep anxiety. Melancholy, because we, all of us—the entire human race—should be grateful to the Greeks and Romans for their contributions to our culture, language, science, and philosophy which became the basis of our civilization. Anxiety, because of the inescapable parallels between those ancient democracies and our current American society.

The downfall of Greek and Roman civilizations was caused by their leaders' greed, and the voting citizens' lack of responsibility. They voted themselves more and more benefits until they emptied their countries' treasuries. When expenses exceeded their ability to collect taxes and continued wars and slavery failed to build sufficient wealth to cover the ever rising benefits, these ancient societies ultimately died. The old adage that those who do not learn from history are bound to repeat it, applies in spades.

Very often contemporaries miss the turning points of history. The depth and historical importance of events is very often not fully recognized in its time. The election of a black President was certainly a historic event. The obvious was recognized and widely celebrated, but the important had been missed. History was not made by the color of the President's skin; it was made by the color of his ideas. In the euphoria of celebration, the ideology of this new President has not been recognized.

Contrary to universal acumen, the Presidency of the United States is not the final destination of Obama's political journey. It is an inflection point to the final destination: the egalitarian dream. Millions of Bolsheviks gave their lives for that dream. Obama is getting there without firing a single shot, making Lenin a historical pigmy.

If Obama's Grand Plan succeeds, this great tragedy will run its predictable course: high taxation, hyperinflation, depleted savings, and the devaluation of the dollar; prolonged economic stagnation and the destruction of our democracy, all culminating in one party rule for all Americans in a social-democratic Obama era.

The upcoming elections are not about Obama or Romney and not about Democrats or Republicans. The elections are not about universal health care, the price of gasoline, or the rate of unemployment. Those variables can be changed and our national debt can still be repaid if we make the right choices and stop taking this democracy for granted.

The issue we face is: What kind of country are we going to be? Whether we remain "one nation under God, indivisible, with liberty and justice for all" or are we going to be "one nation under debt with equality in poverty for all." Whether we are the "Land of the Free" or the "Land of the Voting Herd."

The enemies are at the gates and the fifth column is already inside ready to open the gates to welcome the Marxist socialist future.

The challenge for the American people is to acquire

adequate knowledge, to comprehend the President's agenda and its consequences for the future of this country and for our children and grandchildren. It is imperative for our survival and the preservation of American Idealism.

As Russian journalist Stanislav Mishin wrote after the 2008 elections: "The proud American will descend into slavery without a fight, beating his chest and proclaiming to the world how free he really is."

Mishin could still be proven wrong; Obama's short reign may turn out to be the best thing to happen to this country. The 2008 elections could turn out to be a political wake up call for this nation, like Pearl Harbor or 9/11.

Let us help Obama realize one of his dreams. "I just want to go through Central Park and watch folks passing by. Spend the whole day watching people. I miss that," the President said. We should help the President spend as much time as he wishes in Central Park, sooner rather than later, for the sake of our future.

"You may say I am a dreamer, but I am not the only one"—John Lennon.

Acknowledgements

I was a participant in a wonderful blog, started by my friend Edwig Gershengoren, that debated politics from all points of views, from the furthest left to the hardest right— and we had a great time. Many of the ideas in this book were first tested or developed there, and many of the ideas and much of my inspiration came from the blog. So I want to thank my fellow bloggers for the vigorous discussion that prompted me to use my red communist glasses to analyze the dangers posed to our democracy. I also must thank my wonderful wife, Elena, who allowed me this indulgence to spend nights at the computer rather than in our bed. Finally, I have to thank my daughter Rebecca, my first and best editor, and the person for whom I wrote this book in the hope that the America she raises her children in will be as wonderful to her as it has been to me.

About the Author:

Alexander G. Markovsky, born in the former Soviet Union, is a graduate of both the University of Marxism-Leninism from which he holds degrees in economics and political science as well as from Moscow University, from which he graduated with a degree in engineering. He lives in Houston, Texas, where he runs a consulting company specialized in the management of large international projects. His essays have appeared on RedState.com.

Endnotes

1. The word "Taqiyya" literally means: "Concealing, precaution, guarding." It is employed in disguising one's beliefs, intentions, convictions, ideas, feelings, opinions or strategies. In practical terms it is manifested as dissimulation, lying, deceiving.

2. Pierre-Joseph Proudhon, French politician, philosopher, and socialist, contemporary of Karl Marx

3. Francois Hollande, Socialist and President of France.

4. In 184 7 French politician, philosopher, and socialist Pierre-Joseph Proudhon, criticized Karl Marx's theories in his book "System of Economical Contradictions" or, "The Philosophy of Poverty". In the same year Karl Marx responded to the criticism with his book "The Poverty of Philosophy".

Made in United States
Troutdale, OR
07/03/2023